# Accounting for Equity Compensation

Alan A. Nadel, Thomas M. Haines, and Gregory M. Kopp

**Second Edition (2004)**

# Accounting for Equity Compensation

Alan A. Nadel, Thomas M. Haines, and Gregory M. Kopp

**Second Edition (2004)**

The National Center for Employee Ownership
Oakland, California

**Accounting for Equity Compensation, 2nd ed.**

Alan A. Nadel, Thomas M. Haines, and Gregory M. Kopp

Book design by Scott Rodrick

ISBN: 0-926902-96-2

First printing: March 2003
Second edition, January 2004

The National Center for Employee Ownership
1736 Franklin St., 8th Flr.
Oakland, CA 94612
(510) 208-1300
Fax (510) 272-9510
Email *nceo@nceo.org*
Web *www.nceo.org*

# Contents

# Chapter 1

# Introduction and Background

Our intention in writing this book is to provide equity compensation practitioners with a basic foundation in the financial accounting rules that govern equity compensation programs in the United States. As such, it is geared toward corporate executives who develop, implement and administer equity-based compensation programs as well as attorneys and consultants who advise their clients on stock-based programs.

It is not our intention to provide a complete discussion of all of the relevant accounting rules or to analyze the rules for every conceivable circumstance that may arise. Others have compiled this information for practitioners looking to give expert advice and for those responsible for determining the appropriate financial accounting for corporate equity compensation programs.

## Need for Accounting Guidance

Until the 1960s, there was no formal guidance in accounting literature that specifically addressed the issues relating to equity compensation. In 1972, the Accounting Principles Board (APB) issued Opinion No. 25,

*Accounting for Stock Issued to Employees.* Opinion 25 provided guidance on how businesses in the United States should account for all forms of stock-based compensation that they provided to their employees. At the time, the U.S. economy was in a recession, and the use of stock and stock options as compensatory devices was not as prevalent as it is today. Generally, Opinion 25 provided the necessary guidance that companies were seeking at that time.

During the 1980s, equity compensation became much more widespread, and as the use of stock-based compensation increased, so did the complexity of stock arrangements and planning opportunities. Companies were not only issuing restricted stock and stock options, but also using other equity instruments such as junior stock. Moreover, they were adding features and alternatives to these programs that had not been contemplated when Opinion 25 was developed.

The Financial Accounting Standards Board (FASB), the successor to the Accounting Principles Board, recognized the shortfall between the complexity of equity compensation instruments and the applicable accounting guidance. There was a widespread view that the basic model of Opinion 25 had become flawed in light of the complex arrangements that had come into use. The FASB proposed to develop new guidance that would replace the rather simplified rules of Opinion 25. After some deliberations, however, it was decided in 1987 to postpone this new project indefinitely. By the early 1990s, the FASB realized that the types and nature of equity arrangements in the market far outstripped the available accounting guidance and concluded that it would be necessary to develop new accounting principles that addressed current stock-based compensation arrangements.

In 1993, the FASB issued an Exposure Draft that would significantly alter the way equity arrangements were accounted for in the United States. Under the new approach, companies would be required to recognize an expense for the issuance of all equity awards to employees, a distinct departure from the principles of Opinion 25, which often resulted in no compensation expense for standard stock option grants.

As a result of the Exposure Draft, there was a significant political reaction in the U.S. Congress, and considerable pressure was brought to bear by the business community. There was concern that forcing companies to recognize an expense for all equity grants awarded to employees would have a detrimental effect on corporate America, which in turn would harm the U.S. markets and the U.S. economy. In the end, the FASB finalized the Exposure Draft in the form of FASB Statement No. 123, *Accounting for Stock-Based Compensation.* The most glaring change from the Exposure Draft, however, was the FASB's willingness to make Statement 123 elective rather than required. As discussed in greater detail later in this book, the FASB scaled back its objectives and allowed companies to simply provide footnote disclosure of the accounting impact of implementing the fair value method of Statement 123 for stock-based employee compensation while continuing to use the favorable accounting of Opinion 25. It should be noted that nonemployee awards under Statement 123 were required to be accounted for (not just with footnote disclosures) using the fair value method.

Soon after finalizing Statement 123, the FASB realized that it would be necessary to provide an update to Opinion 25. The FASB initially had intended that Statement 123 would replace Opinion 25, but its conclusion to make the choice optional meant that Opinion 25 would continue to be used by virtually all U.S. companies. Moreover, the high growth in the U.S. stock markets, the continued increase in the use of equity-based compensation for a broader segment of the employee population, and the growing complexities in the types of equity arrangements granted to employees only served to exacerbate the inadequacies of Opinion 25.

In an effort to address the complexities of modern-day compensation arrangements and to reduce the ambiguities in practices that had evolved over the past 30 years, the FASB began a project to provide further guidance under Opinion 25. The effort led to the issuance of FASB Interpretation No. 44, *Accounting for Certain Transactions involving Stock Compensation* ("Interpretation 44"). Although some believe otherwise, Interpretation 44 was meant simply to interpret the principles of Opinion 25 rather than to create new rules.

Even with the issuance of Interpretation 44 in 2000, the FASB recognized the need for more guidance to address the ever-growing complexities of equity arrangements. After much deliberation, the Emerging Issues Task Force (EITF), a standards-setting organization established by the FASB, issued EITF No. 00-23, "Issues Related to the Accounting for Stock Compensation under APB Opinion No. 25 and FASB Interpretation No. 44," a comprehensive volume addressing many of the specific issues stemming from equity arrangements being accounted for under Opinion 25 and using the guidelines of Interpretation 44.

## The Current Environment

As of this writing (December 2003), there has been much turmoil in the U.S. economy. The U.S. stock markets have declined significantly in value, and many companies have discovered accounting irregularities in prior years' financial statements. There have been a number of scandals at major U.S. companies in which senior executives did not act ethically or legally and in certain cases may have manipulated financial statements. The U.S. Congress enacted the Sarbanes-Oxley Act of 2002, a new set of guidelines that raised the bar for corporate governance of U.S. companies. Boards of directors are looking much more closely at their companies, not only for financial performance but also for the integrity and propriety of their management teams and the behavior of their corporate executives. Government regulators such as the Securities Exchange Commission and various state attorneys general have taken aggressive roles in pursuing companies and executives who have acted improperly.

There is a strong perception that a driver for some of today's suspect business practices has been the unbridled growth in the use of equity compensation arrangements that enabled many executives to accumulate massive amounts of wealth. In turn, this was fueled by the size of stock option grants awarded to the executives by companies that could seemingly issue these grants with no financial statement impact as a result of the favorable accounting treatment under Opinion 25.

## The Future

A number of major companies (more than 200 as of December 2003) have announced their intention to adopt Statement 123 and to commence charging an expense to their earnings to reflect the cost of stock options granted to executives and employees. Although the announcements have been general in nature insofar as when and how they intend to implement Statement 123, they have started to spread across a number of different industries. A notable exception has been the technology companies, although Microsoft indicated in July 2003 that it too will begin to recognize an expense for equity grants to its employees. It is still early in the game, and we cannot yet determine whether companies across the board will adopt Statement 123 accounting or whether there will continue to be a mixed bag that intensifies the discrepancies in financial statement reporting.

Notwithstanding the recent business developments in the U.S. and the related corporate announcements, the International Accounting Standards Board (IASB) has proposed new rules that would require companies to recognize an annual expense in their financial statements for option grants to executives and employees. The IASB approach is similar to Statement 123, especially in its methodology for valuing stock options.

Some international companies already follow the IASB's accounting standards, and by 2005, companies throughout the European Union are expected to adopt the IASB's rules. The FASB has indicated a desire to harmonize U.S. accounting standards with those of the IASB so that similar accounting treatment might be accorded to all employee equity compensation programs regardless of the country of their origin.

Furthermore, U.S. legislators have entered the fray to respond to the growing shareholder backlash against the business community. In an attempt to restore confidence in U.S. business and the U.S. capital markets, proposed legislation has been introduced in the U.S. Congress that would require U.S. companies to use accounting treatments similar to Statement 123. Other legislative proposals would penalize companies that do not use Statement 123 accounting or would limit a U.S. tax deduction for stock option exercises to the amount recognized as compensation expense in its financial statements. The FASB itself has signaled its intention to move to an accounting model that would recognize an expense for option grants.

During 2003, the FASB has been actively addressing these issues in order to issue new guidance. The FASB has indicated that it intends to issue proposed guidance in the second quarter of 2004, with final rules issued by the end of the third quarter of 2004 that will take effect for most companies in 2005. There has been ongoing dialogue between the FASB and the IASB, and many practitioners believe that harmonization of the different standards ultimately will be achieved.

Although the FASB has publicized its preliminary conclusions on changes to Statement 123, we have not addressed those changes in this edition of *Accounting for Equity Compensation*. While it is understood that the announced changes will likely be proposed in the near future, they have not in fact been issued for comment or otherwise exposed. Because the FASB can change preliminary conclusions before issuing an exposure draft, and has done so in the past, it would be premature to present those changes until after they are issued in 2004.

Among other changes to Statement 123, the FASB likely will issue new guidance relating to the methodology utilized for valuing stock options. Valuation has been the biggest point of contention and will probably be the issue drawing the most attention once the Exposure Draft is issued. Already different stakeholders have taken an active role in addressing the issue of option valuation and it is expected that the volume will increase with time.

Whatever the final outcome of these developments, the FASB has indicated that it intends to require companies to recognize an expense for option grants. Regardless of legislative proposals that will be enacted, there is growing business pressure and shareholder resolve for companies to use Statement 123. Although shareholders usually have an unfavorable reaction to low earnings, there is a belief that expensing options will result in improved transparency for compensation programs as well as greater accountability. The shareholder voices currently urging companies to recognize compensation expense under Statement 123 will likely put most companies "over the top" and compel them to begin expensing stock option grants.

As a sign of impending change, in December 2002 the FASB issued Statement 148, an amendment to Statement 123 that would provide companies with two additional transition alternatives when changing their accounting policy for stock-based employee compensation from Opinion 25's intrinsic value method to Statement 123's fair value method. The proposals that FASB has been discussing since the issuance of Statement 148 go even further in addressing when and how companies should transition to the new rules.

Statement 123 originally required that its fair value model be applied only to employee awards granted, modified, or settled after the date of adoption. One of the reasons for this transition approach was concern that companies would not be able to estimate the fair values (i.e., using the Black-Scholes or the Binomial Model) of previous option grants. At the time Statement 123 was first adopted, estimation of fair value for previous grants would have been a major issue because such estimation was a new concept for virtually all public companies. Now, however, this is no longer the case. Although relatively few companies have actually adopted Statement 123 to measure expense for their stock option grants, all of them estimate the fair value (generally using the Black-Scholes formula) for their option grants in order to make the footnote disclosures that are required for companies continuing to use Opinion 25. With the issuance of Statement 148, the FASB either is indicating that it anticipates that a significant number of companies will adopt Statement 123 accounting or it intends to encourage more companies to adopt Statement 123.

In contrast to those companies who have announced their intention to adopt Statement 123, others have indicated their strong opposition to any change. Because of the FASB's position, it is anticipated that a successor statement to Statement 123 will be required commencing in 2005. Of course, most companies continue to account for their equity programs under Opinion 25 until new rules are finalized. Thus, it is important not to forget the principles of Opinion 25 and the various interpretations issued in recent years under those principles.

The following chapters provide a more in-depth discussion of the principles, guidance, and interpretations mentioned above. Specifically, we explain the application and provisions of Opinion 25 and Statement 123, including recent interpretations and guidance provided under Interpretation 44 and EITF 00-23. This edition of the book also includes an index.

# Chapter 2

# Introduction to Opinion 25 and Earnings per Share

## Introduction to the Basic Rules of Opinion 25

Opinion 25 was issued in 1972 and applies to stock compensation granted to *employees*. This chapter explains the basic principles and provisions of Opinion 25 and provides the foundation to understand the recently published (and more complex) guidance provided by Interpretation 44 and EITF 00-23.

Opinion 25 uses the "intrinsic value method." Under the intrinsic value method, compensation expense is determined on the measurement date (i.e., the time that both the exercise price and the number of shares are fixed and determinable). The compensation expense is equal to the excess of the fair market value of the stock over the exercise price on the measurement date. For example, assume a standard stock option is granted to an employee with an exercise price of $10.00 on a day when the fair market value of the stock is $14.00 per share. Assuming that the measurement date is the grant date (which normally is the case), the intrinsic value results in $4.00 of compensation expense.

The following key accounting issues must be addressed to analyze the accounting impact of stock-based compensation awards granted to employees:

1. Is the award granted to an employee?
2. Are the stock-based awards compensatory?
3. When should the compensation expense be measured?
4. How should the expense be measured?
5. When should the expense be recognized?
6. How do plan or award modifications impact the accounting?

## 1. Is the Award Granted to an Employee?

Opinion 25 clearly states that the Opinion only pertains to arrangements involving employees. Grants to customers, vendors, lenders, and so on are outside the scope of the Opinion and should be accounted for in accordance with Statement 123 (see chapter 5). The issue of determining who qualifies as an employee is critical to the analysis of determining compensation expense. Accordingly, as organizational structures and alliances became more complex, the need for clarity and guidance on the definition of "employee" became necessary. The additional guidance was provided in Interpretation 44. Although covered in more detail in chapter 3, Interpretation 44 essentially adopts a common-law approach to the definition of "employee" and concludes that an individual is an employee of a grantor if the grantor exercises or has the right to exercise sufficient control over that individual to establish an employer-employee relationship.

## 2. Are the Stock-Based Awards Compensatory?

*Noncompensatory Arrangements*

Most of the guidance provided under Opinion 25 is geared to programs that are deemed to be compensatory. The first step in applying Opinion 25 is to ascertain whether an arrangement may be viewed as being noncompensatory and thus by definition result in no compensation expense. An arrangement will be deemed to be noncompensatory if it meets the following conditions:

1. Only employer stock may be issued.

2. Substantially all full-time employees must be eligible to participate in the plan.

3. Options or awards are granted to eligible employees equally or based on a uniform percentage of salary.

4. The discount from market price at the date the option or award is granted is no greater than the discount that would be reasonable in an offer to stockholders or others. Interpretation 44 confirmed that the maximum discount under Opinion 25 was to be consistent with the federal income tax requirements for a noncompensatory plan under Section 423 of the Internal Revenue Code (the "Code"). Accordingly, the maximum discount permitted under Section 423 of the Code of 15% is the maximum acceptable discount permitted under Opinion 25.

5. The exercise period must be limited to a reasonable period if the plan is in the form of an option. Similarly, in practice, companies have again relied on the specific requirements of Section 423 to define a reasonable period to exercise. Under Section 423, the term of an option generally may not exceed 27 months. A longer term of up to five years is permitted only for options whose strike price is not determined until the date of exercise.

Generally, the only plans that meet these requirements are employee stock purchase plans (ESPPs), and in particular those ESPPs that are qualified under Section 423 of the Code (also known as "Section 423 plans").

Additional analysis under Opinion 25 is not necessary in the instances where a compensation program is deemed to be noncompensatory. Assuming a company accounts for its stock-based compensation programs under Opinion 25, a plan meeting these requirements will be deemed to be noncompensatory and thus will result in no charge to earnings in the company's financial statements.

### Compensatory Arrangements

Aside from employee stock purchase plans, essentially all of the stock-based compensation programs used by companies do not satisfy the conditions of a noncompensatory plan under Opinion 25 and, as such, are deemed to be compensatory. Traditional stock option awards that are prevalent in industry today do not satisfy all of the noncompensatory conditions and are accounted for as compensatory plans. Compensation cost for stock-based awards that are compensatory under Opinion 25 must be measured (although the measured compensation expense may be $0). As previously indicated, the compensation expense, if any, will be based on the value of the shares on the measurement date less any purchase price to be paid by the employee.

## 3. When Should the Compensation Expense Be Measured?

The *measurement date* is the date on which the compensation expense can be determined with certainty. Pursuant to Opinion 25, the measurement date for determining compensation expense for stock options, stock award plans, and other related programs is the first date on which are known both (1) the number of shares that an individual employee is entitled to receive and (2) the option or purchase price to be paid by the employee, if any.

The measurement date for many grants occurs on the date of grant, as is the case with most standard stock options (both the number of shares and the exercise price are known on the date of grant). When the measurement date occurs on the date of grant, the plan is known as a "fixed" plan because the compensation expense, if any, is determined and fixed on that date.

If either the number of shares or the exercise price are not determinable on the date of grant, the plan is referred to as a "variable" plan because the compensation cost is remeasured at each reporting date until it becomes fixed (that is, compensation expense varies based on changes in the underlying stock price). Most companies prefer to avoid the earnings volatility that results from variable plans, and, as such, variable plan accounting is considered less favorable accounting. There are many intentional, and, unfortunately, unintentional plan designs and modifications that can create variable accounting treatment. Because of the adverse impact of variable accounting, compensation professionals should exercise caution before implementing a plan that could result in variable accounting treatment. Examples of variable plans are stock option plans with a variable exercise price, programs with performance-based vesting of awards, and variable cash bonuses that are linked to the exercise of an option (essentially a reduction of exercise price).

### Fixed Plans

The defining feature of a fixed plan is the ability to identify, at the date of grant, both the number of shares of stock that may be acquired by an employee and the amount of cash, if any, to be paid by the employee. For example, a standard stock option award on 100 shares of company stock granted to an employee with a fixed exercise price would generally be considered a fixed award (this assumes that there are no performance-based features attached to the number of shares that are granted or that may vest, or that may vary the exercise price). In this case, the measurement date will occur on the date of grant and will not be adjusted for future company performance or stock price changes.

### Variable Plans

Variable plans have characteristics that prevent a company from determining at the date of grant either the number of shares of stock that may be acquired by an employee or the price to be paid by the employee, or both. Plan designs that use performance conditions other than employee service are accounted for as variable plans. For example, a stock option plan that requires certain performance goals to be attained in order for the employee to vest in the award will be considered a variable plan. As such, compensation expense is remeasured at each reporting date from the date of grant until the necessary terms are fixed and determinable.

## 4. How Should the Compensation Expense Be Measured?

Opinion 25 is based on the intrinsic value method. Accordingly, compensation expense is based on the intrinsic value of the award on the measurement date. On that date, Opinion 25 specifies that compensation expense is equal to the fair market value of the stock at the measurement date less the amount, if any, that the employee is required to pay.

If a fair market value is not available (for example, in a private company), the best estimate of the fair value of the stock should be used. The valuation cannot be reduced to reflect any restrictions or liquidity discounts. This will generally require valuations by appraisers, investment bankers, or valuation experts.

## 5. When Should the Expense Be Recognized?

Opinion 25 states that the company should accrue compensation expense in each reporting period during the service period. If the measurement date is after the grant date, it is necessary to begin accruing compensation expense each period from the date of grant to the date of measurement based on the fair market value of the stock at the end of each reporting period. This approach requires estimates to be made that will subsequently be revised based on actual results.

Accordingly, the following basic principles should be considered when recognizing compensation expense:

- Compensation expense should be charged to expense over the expected service period (the periods in which the employee has performed or will perform services). In the majority of grants, the award is made for future services; accordingly, this period is equal to the vesting period.
- If the awards were granted for past service, the compensation expense should be fully expensed in the period the options are granted or the stock is awarded.

### Recognizing Compensation Expense for a Variable Plan

Opinion 25 states that a company is required to measure compensation expense for all awards in an amount equal to the value by which the fair market value of the shares exceeds the exercise price or amount to be paid by the employee. It is important to note that the measurement date for a variable plan is not the grant date. The compensation expense will be remeasured each period based on the changes (upward and downward, but not below the exercise price) in the fair market value. This approach is commonly referred to as "mark to market" or "mark to intrinsic value" accounting. FASB Interpretation No. 28, *Accounting for Stock Appreciation Rights and Other Variable Stock Option Award Plans* ("Interpretation 28") provides guidance on how to measure and recognize compensation associated with variable plans. Consequently, for variable plans:

- If portions of the award vest at different dates (i.e. graded vesting), each portion is accounted for as a separate award and recognized over the period appropriate to that portion so that compensation expense for each portion should be recognized in full by the time that portion vests.

- When the number of shares is not known, accrual of the compensation expense, if any, should be based on the best available estimate of the number of options or other equity awards that are expected to vest. This estimate should be revised when more reliable estimates of actual data becomes available.

- The fair market value at each reporting period (e.g., the end of a quarter for a public company) must be used to estimate compensation expense. It is not acceptable to estimate what the share price will be at the measurement date.

## Recognizing Compensation Expense for Fixed Plans

For a fixed award, compensation expense may be recognized in the aggregate on a straight-line basis or by some other systematic and rational method over the total service period. Fixed awards with graded vesting may be recognized on a straight-line basis or using the accelerated approach required for a variable award, but cumulative compensation expense for an award at any date can be no less than the expense associated with the vested portion of the award.

## Effect of Forfeiture

Employees may lose the benefit of awards for a variety of reasons, such as termination of employment or target performance criteria not being achieved.

Opinion 25 provides that if an employee forfeits an award solely due to termination of employment, any compensation expense previously

*Reversed own on Termination*

recognized is reversed to income in the period of termination (regardless of whether the plan is fixed or variable).

Compensation expense previously recognized should not be reversed in any other circumstances involving the expiration or cancellation of a fixed award. If an award expires unexercised or is canceled for any reason other than forfeiture, any compensation expense previously recognized should not be adjusted.

### 6. How Do Plan or Award Modifications Impact the Accounting?

The FASB has spent a considerable amount of time addressing ambiguities in practice with regard to plan and award modifications. New and unforeseen plan designs and market volatility created numerous opportunities for accounting inconsistencies between companies and advisors. This is a very complex subject and can result in unintended accounting consequences that can have an adverse impact on a company's financial statements. Minor changes can convert a fixed stock option (with no compensation expense) into an award that requires variable accounting and has the potential for open-ended compensation expense exposure.

Interpretation 44 and EITF 00-23 (covered in detail in chapters 3 and 4 respectively) were prepared to provide accounting guidance for many forms of award modifications. The plan design and award modifications can be as seemingly innocuous as withholding shares beyond the maximum statutory level to satisfy tax liabilities to the more vigorously debated practice of repricing stock options, both of which will generally result in variable accounting. Accordingly, it is important to conduct a comprehensive accounting analysis using all of the accounting guidance and literature before implementing or modifying a stock-based plan or award.

# Application of APB Opinion No. 25 to Common Stock-Based Employee Awards

## Fair Market Value Stock Options

A fair market value stock option is the most common stock-based incentive granted by employers today. Stock options are being granted more deeply into organizations, with many companies granting stock options to all employees. Stock options have also become commonplace incentives for middle management employees and above.

In the basic structure, which is also the most commonly used, a company grants a stock option to an employee to purchase a fixed number of company shares over a predetermined period of time (typically 10 years) with an exercise price equal to the fair market value of the stock on the date of grant.

Stock options are generally granted to employees in exchange for future services. Accordingly, in the typical situation, the employee becomes vested at the end of a designated vesting period (e.g., five-year cliff vesting) or the award vests ratably over the vesting period (e.g., 20% per year). Generally, the employee is eligible, although not required, to exercise the stock option as soon as it becomes vested.

### *Example: Fair Market Value Stock Option*

1. Company A grants a stock option to Employee X to purchase 100 shares of Company A stock on January 1, 2002
2. Exercise price on date of grant = $25
3. Fair market value of the stock on the date of grant = $25
4. All stock options vest on the fourth anniversary of the date of grant
5. Not all employees are eligible to participate

- *Compensatory or Noncompensatory*
  - This fact pattern would not satisfy the requirements of a non-compensatory plan, (e.g., not all employees are eligible to receive awards); therefore, the plan is compensatory.
- *Measurement Date*
  - Under this fact pattern, the measurement date is the grant date (January 1, 2002) because both the number of shares and the exercise price per share are known and "fixed" on that date.
- *Compensation Expense Measurement*
  - On the measurement date, compensation expense is equal to the difference between the fair market value of the stock on the

date of grant and the exercise price to be paid by the employee. In this example, the intrinsic value is $0 (fair market value of the stock is $25 minus the exercise price of $25 = $0).

— Because the fair market value is the same as the exercise price in this plan design, no compensation expense is recognized.

— If the exercise price is less than the fair market value of the stock on the date of grant, compensation expense is recognized (see the following example).

• *Period of Expense Recognition*

— When the option price equals or exceeds the fair market value of the stock on the date of grant, the issue of expense recognition is irrelevant since there is no compensation expense to be recognized in the financial statements. If there was compensation expense, it would be necessary to recognize the compensation expense over the vesting or service period (for future service) or immediately for awards with no service requirements or granted for past service.

### Example: Discounted Stock Option Grant

Employee X receives a stock option to purchase 100 shares of Company A on January 1, 2002, at $20 per share. The fair market value of Company A stock on January 1, 2002, is $25 per share. The options become exercisable on the fourth anniversary of the date of grant (December 31, 2005). Employee X is not entitled to vest in the option if he terminates his service before the end of the vesting period.

• *Conclusions*

— The option grant is compensatory.

— The measurement date for this award is the grant date because both the number of shares and the price per share are known on the date of grant.

— The compensation expense for the discounted stock option is shown below:

| | |
|---|---|
| Fair market value at measurement date | $25 |
| Exercise price | $20 |
| Intrinsic value or spread per share | $ 5 |
| Total number of shares | 100 |
| Fixed compensation expense | $500 |

— The compensation is recognized in a systematic and rational manner over the four-year vesting period. A straight-line expense allocation would result in $125 of compensation expense per year.

— If the employee terminated before the end of Year 4, causing the option to be forfeited, cumulative compensation expense is reversed.

## Restricted Stock Awards

Restricted stock awards are grants of stock to employees, usually at no cost to the employee. Similar to stock options, restricted stock awards typically have a vesting schedule, so the award is contingent on the employee providing future services for the employer. As such the accounting principles for restricted share awards are very similar to that of stock options (with the exception of the $0 exercise price or cost to the employee). In some respects, restricted stock is the ultimate discounted stock option.

*Example: Restricted Stock Award*

1. Company A grants a restricted stock award for 100 shares to Employee X on January 1, 2002

2. No cost to the employee

3. Fair market value of the stock on the date of grant = $25

4. All restricted shares vest on the fourth anniversary of the date of grant

5. Not all employees are eligible to participate

- *Compensatory or Noncompensatory*
  - This fact pattern would not satisfy the requirements of a non-compensatory plan (e.g., not all employees are eligible to receive awards); therefore, the plan is compensatory.

- *Measurement Date*
  - The measurement date is the grant date (January 1, 2002) because both the number of shares and the exercise price or cost per share are known and "fixed" at that date.

- *Compensation Expense Measurement*
  - On the measurement date, compensation expense is equal to the difference between the fair market value of the stock on the date of grant minus the exercise price or cost to be paid by the employee. In this case, the intrinsic value is $25 (the fair market value of the stock is $25 minus the exercise price/cost to employee of $0 = $25) per share, for a total compensation expense of $2,500. It should be mentioned that the FASB does not allow companies to reduce the fair market value of the restricted stock to account for any vesting restrictions. Accordingly, the full fair market value of the stock (e.g., as quoted on an exchange) is used for accounting purposes.

- *Period of Expense Recognition*
  - As a general rule, restricted stock will almost always result in compensation expense. For this example, it will be necessary to recognize the compensation expense of $2,500 over the vesting or service period of four years. Similar to the discounted stock option example, the compensation expense is recognized in a systematic and rational manner over the four-year vesting period. A straight-line expense allocation would result in $625 of compensation expense per year.

## Stock Appreciation Rights

From an economic standpoint, stock appreciation rights (SARs) resemble stock options except that upon exercise, instead of paying cash and receiving stock, the employee receives the intrinsic spread in the form of cash (some SARs provide for delivery of shares with a fair value equal to the intrinsic spread). SARs are structured similarly to stock options, with a predetermined number of shares underlying the awards, an exercise or strike price, a vesting schedule, and a term. The difference is the SAR's net cash payment element. SARs were often granted to provide funding for stock option exercises, so an executive might exercise SARs and stock options simultaneously and use the SAR cash payment to fund the stock option exercise. SARs are flexible and can be structured to pay in stock to the employee or in a combination of cash and stock. The accounting treatment below is for a stand-alone SAR (a SAR that is not granted with a stock option). The accounting treatment for a tandem SAR (a SAR granted with a stock option) is explained after this section.

## Accounting Treatment

In the case of a SAR, the amount the employee must pay (zero) is known at the grant date, but the ultimate measurement of the aggregate amount of compensation must wait until the employee exercises his or her right under the stock appreciation plan. Measurement of the aggregate compensation is equal to the cash and/or fair market value of the stock received at that time.

While a SAR is outstanding, the ultimate amount of compensation is not determinable. As stated previously in this chapter, Opinion 25 and FASB Interpretation No. 28, *Accounting for Stock Appreciation Rights and Other Variable Stock Option or Award Plans*, require interim calculations of the amount of compensation inherent in the SAR that is accounted for as a variable plan. The compensation amount is equal to the number of stock appreciation rights multiplied by the excess of the fair market value over the exercise price.

FIN 28 states that the measurement should be made at the end of each reporting period based on the current market price of the stock. The company will continue to remeasure compensation expense until the SARs are exercised.

There are differences in the accounting for awards subject to cliff vesting and ratable vesting, which are illustrated below.

*Example: Cliff Vesting (no vesting until the end of a designated period)*

The company grants SARs to certain employees on January 1, 2002, based on 10,000 shares. The exercise price is equal to the fair market value on the date of grant, which is $10.

The SARs vest fully at the end of a three-year vesting period, subject to continued employment. At the end of the period, the employee can exercise his or her rights and receive in cash the difference between the fair market value on the date of exercise and the exercise price. The SARs must be exercised by the fifth anniversary of the date of grant.

The final measurement date occurs when the SARs are exercised because this is the date that the number of shares or amount of cash to be delivered upon settlement is known. However, to determine the amount of expense that must be recognized before exercise, the vesting status is considered.

In this example, cliff vesting occurs at the end of year 3, requiring an assumption that one-third of the amount of compensation is recognized as an expense in the first year. The same calculation is made during years 2 and 3 of the vesting cycle. The compensation expense continues to be measured until the SARs are exercised. See table 2-1.

*Example: Vesting Occurs Ratably*

The assumptions are identical to the SAR plan discussed in the previous example, except that the shares/SARs vest ratably over a three-year period (i.e., 33¹/₃% per year).

Generally, the service period is equal to the vesting period; however, with ratable vesting, each vesting tranche is expensed individually as if each vesting tranche was a separate grant.

The aggregate cumulative percentage of compensation cost accrued by the end of each vesting period is as in table 2-2.

Accordingly, the awards that vest in year 1 are assumed to have a one-year service period and therefore are fully expensed in year 1 and continue to accrue compensation expense, if any, over years 2 and 3. The awards the vest in year 2 are deemed to have a two-year service period and are expensed 50% in year 1 and 50% in year 2, and continue to accrue compensation expense, if any, over years 2 and 3. The last vesting cycle is expensed over the three-year service period, with compen-

**Table 2-1**

| | Year | | | |
|---|---|---|---|---|
| | 1 | 2 | 3 | 4 |
| Exercise price | $10 | $10 | $10 | $10 |
| Fair market value | $12 | $14 | $13 | $20 |
| Spread | $2 | $4 | $3 | $10 |
| Total SARs/shares granted | 100,000 | 100,000 | 100,000 | 100,000 |
| Aggregate compensation | $200,000 | $400,000 | $300,000 | $1,000,000 |
| Cumulative % accrued | 33.33% | 66.67% | 100.00% | 100.00% |
| Cumulative expense | $66,667 | $266,667 | $300,000 | $1,000,000 |
| Expense previously recognized | 0 | $66,667 | $266,667 | $300,000 |
| Expense for year | $66,667 | $200,000 | $33,333 | $700,000 |

**Table 2-2**

| Vesting | Year | | | Explanation |
|---|---|---|---|---|
| | 1 | 2 | 3 | |
| Rights vested in Year 1 | 100% | 100% | 100% | Service period equal to 1 year; begin full expensing in year 1 |
| Rights vested in Year 2 | 50% | 100% | 100% | Service period equal to 2 years; begin full expensing over years 1 and 2 |
| Rights vested in Year 3 | 33% | 66% | 100% | Service period equal to 3 years; begin full expensing over years 1, 2, and 3 |
| Subtotal | 183% | 266% | 300% | |
| Annual Cumulative Expense % | 61% | 89% | 100% | Subtotal divided by 3-year vesting period |
| Annual Expense % | 61% | 28% | 11% | |

sation expense accruing over the period equal to 33$^{1}/_{3}$% annually. Compensation cost would be measured as table 2-3.

## Tandem Stock Appreciation Rights

SARs are often granted in tandem with stock options. Generally, when one award is exercised (the SAR or the stock option), the other award is cancelled. If the SAR is exercised, the employee will receive cash from the company and the related stock option will be cancelled. Conversely, if the stock option is exercised, the employee will receive the share of stock and the SAR will be cancelled.

### *Accounting Treatment*

The company must determine the likelihood of each award being exercised. The presumption pursuant to the accounting literature is that the SAR will be exercised, because it allows the employee to participate in the appreciation without any cash outlay.

Accordingly, the accounting treatment is the same as for a standalone SAR: variable accounting is required until the SAR is exercised. This presumption can be rebutted in the unlikely event that the company can show that historically employees have elected to exercise the stock option, which cancels the related SAR.

## Performance Share Awards

Performance share awards are contingent grants of company stock that vest based on the achievement of pre-determined performance criteria. For example, Employee X will have the right to vest in and receive 500 shares of Company A stock if the three-year EPS growth is equal to 20%. If EPS growth is 15%, Employee X will vest in 250 shares, and if the EPS growth is 30%, the number of shares that Employee X will be entitled to vest in will increase to 1,000.

### *Example: Performance Share Award*

1. Company A grants a performance share award to Employee X on January 1, 2002
2. No cost to the employee

**Table 2-3**

| | Year | | | |
|---|---|---|---|---|
| | 1 | 2 | 3 | 4 |
| Exercise price | $10 | $10 | $10 | $10 |
| Fair market value | $12 | $14 | $13 | $20 |
| Spread | $2 | $4 | $3 | $10 |
| Total SARs/shares granted | 100,000 | 100,000 | 100,000 | 100,000 |
| Aggregate compensation | $200,000 | $400,000 | $300,000 | $1,000,000 |
| Cumulative % accrued | 61.00% | 89.00% | 100.00% | 100.00% |
| Cumulative expense | $122,000 | $356,000 | $300,000 | $1,000,000 |
| Expense previously recognized | 0 | $122,000 | $356,000 | $300,000 |
| Expense for year | $122,000 | $234,000 | ($56,000) | $700,000 |

3. Fair market value of the stock on the date of grant = $10
4. Number of shares that vest to Employee X will depend on the company's EPS growth at the end of a three-year period
5. Not all employees are eligible to participate

**Table 2-4. Performance Share Matrix**

| Three-Year EPS Growth % | Shares Earned |
|---|---|
| Less than 15% | 0 |
| 15%–19% | 250 |
| 20%–29% | 500 |
| 30%+ | 1,000 |

- *Compensatory or Noncompensatory*
  - This is a compensatory plan. It does not satisfy all of the requirements of a noncompensatory plan.
- *Measurement Date*
  - In this example, the measurement date is not known on the date of grant because the number of shares is not fixed on the date of grant. Therefore this plan is subject to variable accounting treatment. The compensation expense will be determined on the measurement date (the date that both the exercise price, if any, and the number of shares are fixed and determinable). Until that date, Company A will use "mark to market" accounting and will recognize compensation expense that will vary with the performance expectations and the stock price for each interim measurement period.
- *Compensation Expense Measurement and Period of Expense Recognition*
  - The company is required to account for this program using variable accounting. The company cannot fully calculate the compensation expense until the performance shares are earned, if any, by Employee X. In the reporting periods leading up to that measurement date at the end of the three-year performance period, the company will use "mark to market" accounting to measure compensation expense and will recognize compensation expense pursuant to FIN 28.

In the first year, the EPS growth is 20%, so it is estimated that 500 shares will be issued to Employee X at the end of the performance period. The stock price on that reporting date is $10 per share. Accordingly, the estimated compensation expense for the award is $5,000. One-third of the award is vested as of that date, so the company must recognize expense of $1,665.

In the second year, EPS growth decreases to 15%. Based on the performance share matrix, it is estimated that only 250 shares will ultimately be issued to Employee X at the end of the performance period. The stock price on that reporting date is $12 per share. Accordingly, the company's total expense has been revised downward to $3,000. Employee X is two-thirds vested in the award, so the company must recognize additional expense of $335 (two-thirds × $3,000 - $1,665 of expense that was already recognized).

In the final year, EPS growth increases to 30%. Based on the performance share matrix, it is determined that the maximum number of shares of 1,000 will be awarded to Employee X. This is the *measurement date* (both the number of shares and cost to the employee are known and determinable). The stock price on that measurement reporting date is $15 per share. Accordingly, the company's total expense has been revised upward to $15,000. Employee X is fully vested in the award, so the company must recognize additional expense of $13,000 (three-thirds × $15,000 - $2,000 of expense that was already recognized). (See table 2-5.)

**Table 2-5**

| Calculation | Years | | |
|---|---|---|---|
| | 1 | 2 | 3 |
| EPS Growth | 20% | 15% | 30% |
| Stock Market Value | $10.00 | $12.00 | $15.00 |
| Shares Issuable | 500 | 250 | 1,000 |
| Aggregate Compensation Expense | $5,000 | $3,000 | $15,000 |
| Cumulative % Earned | 33% | 67% | 100% |
| Cumulative Compensation Expense | $1,665 | $2,000 | $15,000 |
| Expense Previously Recognized | $0 | $1,665 | $2,000 |
| Compensation Expense for Year | $1,665 | $335 | $13,000 |

## Qualified Employee Stock Purchase Plans (Section 423 Plans)

Employee stock purchase plans are designed to promote a broad-based employee ownership culture by providing employees with the ability to purchase stock, often at a discount from the fair market value. When tax-qualified, these plans are also commonly referred to as Section 423 plans (because they are designed to achieve certain tax benefits provided by Section 423 of the Code).

Under the standard plan design, employees can purchase company stock at a discount of up to 15% from the fair market value of the stock (a discount exceeding 15% would create a compensatory plan and would result in compensation expense for financial reporting purposes). The plan term often runs for a 12-month period, but can vary as long as it does not exceed 27 months (a period of five years is permitted only for options whose strike price is not determined until the date of exercise). For example:

1. Employee participates in the company employee stock purchase plan
2. All employees are eligible to participate in the plan
3. Employee contributes 5% of pay to the plan (resulting in a contribution of $500 per month)
4. The plan term is 12 months
5. At the end of the 12-month period, the stock is trading at $50 per share
6. The stock purchase price is equal to 85% of the fair value of the stock on the purchase date

At the end of the plan term, the employee has contributed a total of $6,000 to the ESPP and has the ability to purchase company stock at a price of $42.50 per share (85% × $50 per share = $42.50). The employee would purchase 141 shares of common stock (141 shares × $42.50 = $5,992.50). The remaining $7.50 would typically be redistributed to the employee in cash.

Under this arrangement, the plan would be noncompensatory and would not result in any compensation expense.

For reference, the rules under Code Section 423 provide that:

1.  The stock purchase price may not be less than the lesser of (a) 85% of the fair market value of the stock when the option is granted or (b) 85% of the fair market value of the stock at exercise or purchase date.

2.  The maximum option life is five years from the grant date if the option price is not less than 85% of the fair market value of the stock at date of exercise. If the option price is stated in any other terms (such as a look-back option), the maximum option life is 27 months from the grant date.

3.  The option or right to purchase stock must be granted to all employees, except part-time employees (20 hours or less weekly or not more than five months a year), employees with less than two years' service, and highly compensated employees (as defined by Code Section 414).

4.  All employees must have the same rights and privileges, except that the amount of stock any employee may purchase may be a uniform percentage of compensation, and the plan may limit the maximum number of shares any one employee may purchase.

5.  Owners of 5% or more of the value or voting power of all classes of stock of the employer or its parent or subsidiary may not participate.

6.  No employee may be able to purchase more than $25,000 of stock in any calendar year.

7.  The option may not be transferable (other than by will or laws of inheritance) and may be exercisable only by the employee to whom it is granted.

### Qualified Employee Stock Purchase Plans with a Look-Back Option Feature

A look-back option is a variation on the standard ESPP design. This plan allows the employee to purchase the stock at 85% of the lower of the fair market value on (1) the date of grant or (2) the date of purchase. For example, assume the same facts as the example above and also assume the stock was trading at $20 per share on the date of the grant of the rights (the commencement of the plan).

The employee can now purchase 352 shares of company stock at a price of $17 per share (85% × $20 stock value). Although this plan allows an employee to purchase stock at a discount considerably greater than 15% of the current fair market value, it is still considered a non-compensatory arrangement under Opinion 25 and results in no compensation expense.

### Example: Look-Back Options

Fair market value, date of grant: $20
Fair market value, date of purchase: $50

Under a look-back option plan, the employee would exercise his or her right to purchase the stock at the end of the term, for example in 12 months, at 85% of the date of grant price, or $17 per share. On the purchase date, the stock trades at $50 per share, so that the stock is sold to the employee at a 66% discount to the current market price.

# Accounting Treatment for Stock Option Exercises and Employee Loans

A problem for employees that want to exercise stock options is the cash outlay that is required for the exercise price and the potential resulting income tax liability. A number of techniques have been developed to assist employees to meet the cash liabilities and/or to maximize the number of shares that the employee retains. This section identifies the most commonly used techniques.

## Stock-for-Stock Exercise (Stock Swap)

In this technique, the employee exercises a stock option by exchanging currently owned shares, rather than cash, for the exercise price.

### Example

An employee owns 1,000 shares of his employer's stock and has a stock option to acquire 1,000 shares at an exercise price of $10 per share. The shares are currently trading at $20 per share. The total cost to the employee (excluding taxes) to exercise the option is $10,000.

Rather than selling his currently owned shares or obtaining other sources of financing, the employee can elect to deliver to his employer 500 shares that he owns as payment for the $10,000 exercise price. In return, the employee will receive 1,000 shares of his employer's stock worth $20,000.

*Accounting Result*   MATURE  SHARES =  Held
                                           6 mos

This technique does not result in any adverse accounting changes and will not alter the existing accounting treatment as long as the shares that are transferred to the company are mature (shares that have been owned by the employee for at least six months). The use of immature shares (holding period of less than six months) will alter the accounting treatment and will result in a new measurement date. This is discussed in the next example.   LESS  6 mos    NEW
                              measurement   DATE

## Stock Option Pyramiding

Stock option pyramiding is the practice of using shares recently acquired by virtue of a stock option exercise and using those shares to satisfy the exercise price on the remaining shares under option.

*Example*

An employee holds an exercisable option to acquire 5,000 shares. The option exercise price is $20 a share (equal to the fair market value of the stock on the date of grant), and the current fair market value of the shares is $25. The employee currently owns 1,000 shares of company stock. The employee has the ability to use the shares that he currently owns to effectively exercise all of the unexercised stock options. For example, assume an initial option exercise for 1,250 shares that is funded by exchanging the 1,000 shares that are owned by the employee. The employee could then immediately exchange the newly acquired 1,250 shares (worth $31,250) to satisfy the $20 exercise price on 1,563 additional option shares. Then the employee could use those 1,563 shares (worth $39,063) to exercise 1,953 option shares (worth $48,828), and use 188 of those shares (worth $4,680) to exercise the final 234 option shares. By doing this, the employee ends up owning 2,000 shares worth $50,000 (table 2-6).

**Table 2-6**

| | Options Exercised | Shares Submitted for Exercise | Shares Owned | Shares Under Option | Value of Shares Owned |
|---|---|---|---|---|---|
| Initial | | | 1,000 | 5,000 | $25,000 |
| Exercise 1 | 1,250 | (1,000) | 1,250 | 3,750 | 31,250 |
| Exercise 2 | 1,563 | (1,250) | 1,563 | 2,188 | 39,063 |
| Exercise 3 | 1,953 | (1,563) | 1,953 | 234 | 48,828 |
| Exercise 4 | 234 | (188) | 2,000 | 0 | 50,000 |
| Totals | 5,000 | (3,000) | 2,000 | 0 | $50,000 |

*PYRAMIDING!  NEW MEASUREMENT DATE C POSSible MEASURID ACCI*

*Accounting Result*

The FASB has stated that this type of transaction is analogous to a stock appreciation right and could result in a new measurement date and, most likely, variable accounting. If the shares used to fund each exercise have been owned by the employee for a period of six months, there is no accounting impact.

If the employee held the shares used to meet the exercise liability for less than 6 months (i.e., immature shares), the pyramiding would result in a new measurement date. In other words, the compensation expense would be equal to the excess of the current fair market value of the stock over the option price at the date of exercise. It is possible that if the shares used to fund all of the exercises were obtained via open market transactions (and not through employee compensation and benefit programs), the pyramiding technique would not result in any compensation expense. Because the employee made an investment in the open market purchases, the structure no longer has the characteristics of a stock appreciation right. Accordingly, the issue arises when employees use the pyramid technique using shares that were obtained through employee compensation and benefit programs. Generally, if an option agreement permits the exercise of options with immature shares, whether through a pyramiding scheme or otherwise, variable accounting is required.

*open mkt shares would not generate*

## Brokerage Arrangement

Many companies have established arrangements with an outside brokerage firm to assist employees in exercising their stock options. The broker receives the exercise instructions, and upon the settlement of the transaction the broker makes payment to the company for the exercise price and withholding taxes, with the balance of the net sales proceeds remitted to the employee.

*Accounting Treatment*

This arrangement, which provides economic benefits to the holder similar to a stock appreciation right, does not require variable accounting or result in a new measurement date because the company does not pay the cash to settle the award. Accordingly, if the company was accounting for the stock option grant as a fixed award, the use of a brokerage arrangement normally does not result in a modification to the accounting treatment.

*Tax Withholding*

An employee may use employer shares that he or she would have otherwise received on exercise to satisfy tax withholding requirements. In essence, the employer repurchases the shares acquired on option exercise from the employee to provide the employee with a means to make the required tax payment. As confirmed under Interpretation 44, a company may withhold option shares to cover tax withholding at the *minimum statutory tax rate* without triggering a new measurement date. An agreement to withhold shares in excess of the statutory minimum withholding on the exercise of a fixed option award triggers variable award accounting for the entire stock option award because the number of shares necessary to meet the tax withholding requirement cannot be determined until the exercise date. Using a brokerage arrangement however, an employee can instruct the broker to withhold (i.e., sell) additional shares in excess of the minimum statutory withholding rate without triggering a new measurement date or variable accounting, because the employer is not providing the proceeds needed to make that payment; rather, the broker provides the proceeds from the sale of the option shares on the open market.

## Loans to Employees to Fund Stock Exercises and Purchases

There are occasions when companies will provide loans to employees to finance the exercise of stock option awards and the income tax liability. The loans can be structured in a number of ways; however, the accounting treatment is dependent upon the substance of the recourse or nonrecourse structure of the note. The substance of the loan should be considered over the form of the loan.

*Nonrecourse Loans*

Loans are sometimes granted to employees to facilitate stock option exercises. A loan is considered nonrecourse when the employee only collateralizes the note with the shares that were received upon exercise. If the value of the shares is less than the amounts due under the loan, the employee can choose to not pay the loan and instead turn over to the company the shares that were obtained via the exercise. The employee's personal assets are not at risk because of the nonrecourse nature of the note.

The EITF concluded in Issue No. 95-16, "Accounting for Stock Compensation Arrangements with Employer Loan Features under APB Opinion No. 25," that a nonrecourse note to purchase stock is analogous to a stock option—that is, the employee does not have any real ownership in the stock because he or she has the ability to turn over the shares to the company and have no further liability if the stock price declines below the purchase price. As such, the employee is in the same economic position as if he or she had not ever purchased the stock.

The loan and outstanding shares are in combination treated as a stock option for accounting purposes. Further, if interest on the note also is nonrecourse, interest is considered part of the exercise price of the options. If the amount of interest due could vary (either because the rate of interest fluctuates or because the "borrower" could prepay the note and pay less interest than if the note was paid at maturity), the exercise price is not known. The transaction results in variable accounting, which is often not the intended consequence, particularly when the stock options that were exercised previously were accounted for as fixed awards. The new option has the following features:

- A term that is the life of the nonrecourse note;

- An exercise price that is made up of the principal and interest due on the note (provided that the interest also is nonrecourse); and

- A number of underlying shares that, in effect, are the same shares that have already been issued in exchange for the nonrecourse note.

There are several circumstances under which a loan that is recourse in form is considered to be a nonrecourse loan for accounting purposes:

- 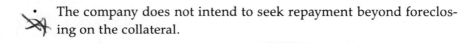 The company does not intend to seek repayment beyond foreclosing on the collateral.

- Historically, the company has not demanded repayment of loan amounts in excess of the collateral.

- The employee does not have sufficient personal assets, other than the shares that are used as collateral, to satisfy the note.

It should also be noted that the purchase of company stock (other than through the exercise of stock options) with a nonrecourse note is also accounted for as a stock option. For example, if a new employee is hired and purchases 10,000 shares of stock on the open market that is funded by a company-provided interest bearing nonrecourse note, the award is deemed to be an option and likely will result in variable accounting treatment (the company has effectively purchased the shares in the market and granted an option to its employee on those same shares).

Accordingly, when a company structures a stock option grant with a nonrecourse note or makes the note available to the employee, the transaction will generally result in variable accounting, which is often not the intended accounting treatment when companies grant stock options. The nonrecourse note principal and/or interest are considered part of the exercise price of a stock option, and therefore the award generally requires variable accounting.

### Recourse Loans

By contrast, if stock options are exercised or stock is otherwise purchased in exchange for a recourse loan to an employee, the exercise or purchase is considered substantive because the employer has recourse to the employee's assets, beyond the purchased securities, and would intend to enforce that right in the event of default by the employee. There is no accounting impact on the stock option exercise or purchase if a recourse note is used to finance the transaction (provided that interest rate on the note is a market rate for the specific borrower). However, the substance of the transaction has to be considered to make the proper assessment. The company must consider:

- Will the full repayment be enforced?

- Has the company historically enforced the repayment of recourse loans from other employees?

- Does the executive have sufficient assets, other than the shares that were purchased with the note, to satisfy the loan?

If the conditions are not satisfied, the note will be considered non-recourse for accounting purposes and, therefore, might result in variable accounting.

*Recourse Note with Below-Market Interest Rates*

An employee stock option that can be exercised with a recourse note that does not bear interest at a market rate generally will result in variable accounting. This is an issue for both fixed interest rates that are below market as of the exercise date as well as variable rate structures that are below market on the date of exercise. Because the fair value of the note is not known until the date of exercise, the exercise price is deemed to be variable, and as a result, variable accounting is required until the award is exercised, forfeited, or expires.

It should be noted that these transactions are complex because the loan structures can take many different forms. Accordingly, there are many factors that should be considered to determine the accounting treatment for a company-provided note issued to purchase company stock. Interpretation 44 and EITF 00-23 cover specific instances and examples in detail and should be reviewed before making an accounting determination.

# FASB Statement No. 128, Earnings per Share

## Overview

The guidance for calculating and presenting earnings per share is provided in FASB Statement No. 128, *Earnings per Share*. Earnings per share is a complex calculation and requires extensive knowledge of accounting procedures and financial statements. This section serves as an introduction to EPS, because it is important for compensation practitioners to understand the EPS impact of equity based compensation; however, a qualified accountant should perform the actual calculation of EPS.

There are two EPS concepts under FASB 128: *Basic EPS,* which is computed by dividing income available to common shareholders by the weighted average number of common shares outstanding for the period, and *Diluted EPS,* which reflects the dilutive impact of all securities that could be converted into common stock (e.g., convertible preferred, convertible debt, employee stock options, convertible warrants).

## Basic EPS

As stated above, Basic EPS is income available to common shareholders divided by the weighted average number of common shares outstanding for the period. It does not include employee stock options and nonvested stock awards (e.g., restricted stock) in the weighted average shares outstanding calculation.

### Example of Basic EPS

> Net Income: $1,500,000
> Weighted Avg. Number of Shares Outstanding: 1,000,000
> Basic EPS: $1.50

Basic EPS would exclude all unearned restricted shares and any unexercised stock options.

### Weighed Average Number of Shares Outstanding

The weighted average number of shares is an average of the shares outstanding during the reporting period used for calculating EPS. The weighted average calculation can be based on a daily average; however, less frequent measurements are acceptable as long is it is reasonable.

Assume that on January 1, 2002, there were 10,000,000 shares outstanding, and the following transactions occurred during the year:

- On February 28, 2002, the company issued 2,500,000 additional shares for cash.
- On June 30, 2002, an additional 1,500,000 shares were issued for cash.

- On September 21, 2002, 1,000,000 shares were repurchased.
- On December 2, 2002, an additional 1,000,000 shares were issued for cash.

The weighted average number of shares calculation for the period were 12,654,795. The calculation is provided in table 2-7.

## Diluted EPS

Diluted EPS measures company performance over a period of time but includes the dilutive impact of all potential common shares in the number of shares outstanding. Potential shares outstanding generally represents all instruments that could be converted into stock at some point in the future. Common examples include stock options, warrants, and convertible securities. The dilutive effect of all unvested shares and stock options is determined using the Treasury Stock Method (described below). Instruments that could be considered antidilutive are excluded. For example, stock options are not include in the shares outstanding calculation if they are out of the money and would be antidilutive (or, in other words, would increase EPS).

The Treasury Stock Method is applied to each award separately as follows:

1. Assume that all option awards or rights are exercised.
2. Calculate the hypothetical proceeds received by the company. The hypothetical proceeds consist of:

   a. The amount to be paid by employees (zero in the case of unvested stock);

   b. The average amount of any unrecognized compensation costs, if any; and

   c. Any tax benefits that would be credited to paid-in capital on exercise. (This situation occurs when a tax deduction for compensation is greater than the compensation cost recognized for financial reporting purposes—for example, a standard nonqualified fair market value stock option.) Incentive stock options are not

**Table 2-7**

| A | B | C | D | E |
|---|---|---|---|---|
| Date | Shares | Days Outstanding | (B) × (C) | Weighted Avg. Shares Outstanding (Sum of (D)/ Days in Period) |
| 01/01/02 | 10,000,000 | 365 | 3,650,000,000 | |
| 02/28/02 | 2,500,000 | 306 | 765,000,000 | |
| 06/30/02 | 1,500,000 | 184 | 276,000,000 | |
| 09/21/02 | (1,000,000) | 101 | (101,000,000) | |
| 12/02/02 | 1,000,000 | 29 | 29,000,000 | |
| **12/31/02** | | **365** | **4,619,000,000** | **12,654,795** |

deductible for tax purposes and do not provide any tax benefit in the calculation.

3. Assume that the hypothetical proceeds are used to buy back shares on the open market at the average stock price for the relevant period.

4. The number of shares issued upon exercise or conversion less the assumed shares repurchased is the net additional shares considered outstanding in the diluted EPS calculation.

Restricted stock that vests solely upon time-based or service-based vesting is considered the equivalent of an option grant with no exercise price. Accordingly, the proceeds are equal to the unrecognized compensation costs (number 2b in the example above) plus any tax benefits that would be credited to paid-in-capital (number 2c in the example above).

Stock options and restricted stock that contain performance-based features (other than time-based vesting and continued employment) are considered Contingently Issuable Shares and are not included in Diluted EPS until the performance criteria are achieved, if it is assumed that the end of the reporting period is the end of the contingency period for the awards (the date at which the performance criteria must be achieved in order for the award to be received, earned or vested, depending on the plan). The objective is to include the awards in Diluted EPS when it appears likely that, based on the status of performance criteria measures, that the shares would be earned as a result of the performance criteria being achieved.

SARs or other awards that may be settled in cash or stock are included in the calculation of Diluted EPS based on the facts and circumstances of the grant. However, the presumption is that the SARs will be settled in stock and the resulting potential common shares will be included in the Diluted EPS calculation, assuming the effect is dilutive. The presumption that the SARs will be settled in cash can be rebutted if the company can demonstrate a history of the awards being settled in cash.

Employee stock options are considered dilutive and therefore included in the denominator only if the average fair market value of the stock during the measurement period is greater than the exercise price of the stock option or other equity instrument. Stock options that meet that requirement are included in the denominator for the period in which they were outstanding.

## Illustration of Treasury Stock Method

Table 2-8 illustrates the Treasury Stock Method. In this example, assume that the company has granted 200,000 stock options with an exercise price of $8 when the underlying stock price was $8 and, therefore, no compensation expense results. Additionally, the average stock price during the measurement period is $10. The corporate tax rate is 35%.

The increase in shares outstanding is a result of the issuance of the 200,000 stock options. Additionally, if the company granted restricted stock that had not yet vested, those shares would be excluded for Basic EPS purposes until they vest, but would be included for the Diluted EPS calculations (provided they are dilutive)

## Example of Diluted EPS Using Diluted Number of Shares Outstanding

Net Income: $1,500,000

Weighted Avg. Number of Shares Outstanding: 1,026,000

Basic EPS: $1.46

Comparing the results of the Basic EPS and the Diluted EPS shows that the issuance of 200,000 options resulted in a $.04 reduction in earnings per share, or a 3% decrease.

**Table 2-8**

| | |
|---|---|
| Weighted average number of shares outstanding (used for basic EPS) | 1,000,000 |
| Number of shares under options with exercise price of $8.00 | 200,000 |
| Number of shares that would have been repurchased at fair value | |
| *Proceeds* | |
|     Hypothetical proceeds from exercise $8.00 ex. price × 200,000 options) | $1,600,000 |
|     Tax benefit ($10.00-$8.00 X 200,000 = $400,000 of compensation × 35%) | $140,000 |
|     Total hypothetical proceeds | $1,740,000 |
|     Number of shares that could be repurchased in the market ($1,740,000/$10.00) | 174,000 |
| | (174,000) |
| Effective net additional shares issued (200,000 - 174,000) | 26,000 |
| Weighted average number of shares and potential common shares used for diluted EPS | 1,026,000 |

# Chapter 3

# Recent Developments Affecting Opinion 25: FASB Interpretation No. 44

After the release of Statement 123, it became clear that additional guidance under Opinion 25 would be necessary. Although the initial intent was for Statement 123 to become the new standard for equity-based compensation accounting, the FASB decided to let employers choose whether to account under Opinion 25 (with footnote disclosures and pro forma Statement 123 costs) or account under Statement 123. Consequently, there was a need for additional guidance.

In March 2000, the FASB issued Interpretation No. 44 ("Interpretation 44"), *Accounting for Certain Transactions Involving Stock Compensation, an Interpretation of APB Opinion No. 25.* Since the issuance of Opinion 25 in 1972, there had been a lack of clarity on its application in certain situations. The ambiguities resulted in confusion and inconsistent application of Opinion 25.

To address the issues and provide the needed guidance, FASB issued Interpretation 44. Among other issues, Interpretation 44 clarifies the application of Opinion No. 25 for (1) the definition of employee for purposes of applying Opinion No. 25, (2) the criteria for determining whether a plan qualifies as a noncompensatory plan, (3) the accounting consequences of various modifications to the terms of a previously fixed stock option or award, and (4) the accounting for an exchange of stock compensation awards in a business combination.

This chapter provides a brief review of the key elements of Opinion 25 and then presents a detailed review and explanation of the issues covered in Interpretation 44.

Interpretation 44 addressed only certain practice issues. Because of the fast-changing business environment and stock market fluctuations, however, Interpretation 44 lacked some of the specificity that was needed. To provide further guidance on the application of Opinion 25, EITF 00-23 was released, which has addressed more than 50 specific issues. See chapter 4 for a detailed review of EITF 00-23.

# Overview of Opinion 25

## In General

APB Opinion No. 25 is the longstanding accounting standard that provides guidance on how companies should account for stock compensation granted to employees; further accounting guidance and clarification of Opinion 25 has been provided over the years through FASB Interpretation No. 28 and numerous issues addressed by the Emerging Issues Task Force (EITF).

## Measurement Date

The fundamental principle underlying Opinion 25 is that compensation cost for stock options or awards is measured at the first date that both the number of shares an employee is entitled to receive and the option or purchase price (if any) are known; this date is referred to as the award's "measurement date."

A new measurement date is generally required if otherwise fixed stock options or awards are modified to "renew" the award or "extend" the exercise period of a stock option.

## Intrinsic Value

The amount of compensation cost (as measured on the measurement date) is equal to the excess of the fair market value of the stock underlying the award over the amount (if any) required to be paid for the award; this excess is referred to as the award's "intrinsic value."

## Fixed Awards

Stock options or awards for which both the number of shares and the option or purchase price (if any) are fixed on the date of grant (or subsequent modification) are referred to as "fixed awards"; examples of fixed awards include time-vesting stock options and restricted stock.

## Variable Awards

Stock options or awards for which either the number of shares or the option or purchase price (if any) are dependent on future events (other than continued service) are referred to as "variable awards"; examples of variable awards include performance-vesting stock options, stock appreciation rights (SARs), and performance shares.

## Recognizing Compensation Cost

Compensation cost is generally recognized ratably over the vesting period, and is reversed only if the stock option or award is forfeited because the employee fails to "fulfill an obligation"; cash or other consideration paid to settle a stock option or award generally represents the final measure of compensation cost.

## If Opinion 25 Does Not Apply

Stock options or awards that are excluded from the scope of Opinion 25 (discussed below) are instead accounted for under the "fair value" provisions of FASB Statement No. 123 (Statement 123) and the measurement date provisions of EITF Issue No. 96-18; these provisions generally require companies to recognize as compensation cost the Black-Scholes or binomial value of stock options and the fair market value (less the purchase price, if any) of other stock-based awards, as measured on the award's *vesting date*.

Compensation cost is generally recognized ratably over the vesting period, with interim fair value accruals between grant and vesting dates based on stock price changes during the period.

# Scope of Opinion 25

## In General

Opinion 25 applies strictly to stock compensation granted (1) by a company with respect to its own stock, and (2) to an "employee" of the grantor company; Opinion 25 does *not* apply to stock compensation granted to individuals who are (1) not employees of the grantor company, (2) employees of a company other than the grantor company, or (3) employees of the grantor company where the stock compensation is based on the stock of another company.

## Definition of Employee

An individual is considered an employee for purposes of Opinion 25 if (1) the individual qualifies as a "common law" employee of the grantor company and (2) if applicable, the grantor company treats the individual as an employee for purposes of U.S. payroll tax compliance (in accordance with the 20-factor guidance provided by Revenue Ruling 87-41); independent contractors and other nonemployee service providers are *not* considered employees for purposes of Opinion 25.

## Exception for Lease or Co-Employment Agreements

An individual who provides services to the grantor company pursuant to a lease or co-employment agreement *may be* considered an employee for purposes of Opinion 25 (even though the grantor/lessee company is not the "employer of record" for purposes of U.S. payroll tax compliance), provided (1) the individual qualifies as a common-law employee of the grantor company and the lessor is contractually obligated to administer payroll taxes, and (2) the lessor and grantor company agree in writing that, among other things, the grantor company has the exclusive right to grant stock compensation to the individual, and the individual has the ability to participate on a "comparable" basis in the grantor company's employee benefit plans.

## Exception for Nonemployee Directors

Although technically not meeting the Opinion 25 definition of employee, Opinion 25 *does* apply to stock compensation granted to a nonemployee member of the grantor company's board of directors for services provided as a director, provided the nonemployee director was either (1) elected by shareholders or (2) appointed to a board position that will eventually be filled by a shareholder election; Opinion 25 does *not* apply to stock compensation granted (1) to individuals who provide advisory or consulting services in a nonelected capacity, such as members of an "advisory board," or (2) to nonemployee directors (even if elected by shareholders) for services outside their role as a director, such as for legal or investment banking advice, or loan guarantees.

## Exception for Consolidated Financial Statements

Opinion 25 does not apply to stock compensation granted to individuals who are employees of a company other than the grantor company; in consolidated financial statements, however, Opinion 25 applies in an "umbrella" fashion to all stock compensation granted by *any member* of a consolidated group to employees of *any other member* of the consolidated group.

That is, Opinion 25 applies in consolidated financial statements to all stock compensation granted by (1) the consolidated parent to employees of any consolidated subsidiary, (2) a consolidated subsidiary to employees of the consolidated parent, and (3) a consolidated subsidiary to employees of any other consolidated subsidiary within the consolidated group.

The underlying rationale for Opinion 25 treatment is that (1) the determination of whether an individual is an employee for purposes of Opinion 25 is made at the consolidated group level and (2) the stock compensation of a subsidiary is deemed to be stock compensation of the consolidated group.

Opinion 25 does not apply to stock compensation granted to employees of a company that is not a member of the consolidated group (such as a joint venture or other equity investment), regardless of whether the stock compensation is granted "downstream" (that is, from the parent to employees of a nonconsolidated subsidiary), "midstream" (that is, from a consolidated subsidiary to employees of a non-consolidated subsidiary, or vice versa), or "upstream" (that is, from a nonconsolidated subsidiary to employees of the parent).

FASB Interpretation No. 44 ("Interpretation 44") does not provide guidance in regard to how a grantor company is to account for stock compensation granted to employees of a nonconsolidated company, but the EITF has concluded that the fair value of the stock compensation (as ultimately measured on the award's vesting date) is recognized as compensation cost over the service period with an offsetting contribution to capital (EITF Issue No. 00-12). Interpretation 44 also does not provide guidance in regard to how to account for a stock option that is based on the stock of an unrelated entity, but the EITF has concluded that the fair value of such an option award should be accounted for as a "derivative" under FASB Statement No. 133 in the determination of net income (both during and subsequent to vesting) (EITF Issue No. 02-08 and Issue 00-23, Issue 51).

## Exception for Separate Financial Statements of a Consolidated Subsidiary

Except for the special rules dealing with consolidated financial statements, Opinion 25 does not apply to stock compensation based on the stock of a company other than the grantor company; in the *separate financial statements of a consolidated subsidiary*, however, Opinion 25 *does* apply to stock compensation granted by the consolidated parent to employees of the consolidated subsidiary.

Opinion 25 applies (1) *only if* the subsidiary is consolidated with the parent and (2) *only to* stock compensation granted by the consolidated parent to employees of the consolidated subsidiary.

Opinion 25 does *not* apply to stock compensation granted (1) to employees of the consolidated subsidiary by another subsidiary of the consolidated group or (2) by the consolidated subsidiary to employees of the parent or any other subsidiary of the consolidated group.

Interpretation 44 does not provide guidance in regard to how a subsidiary is to separately account for stock compensation granted to its employees by a company other than the consolidated parent (such as a nonconsolidated company or a consolidated company other than the parent), but the EITF has concluded that the fair value of the stock compensation (as ultimately measured on the award's vesting date) is recognized as compensation cost over the service period with an offsetting contribution to capital (EITF Issue No. 00-12 and 00-23, Issue 22); Interpretation 44 also does not provide guidance in regard to how a subsidiary is to separately account for stock compensation granted to employees of another member of the consolidated group (other than the grantor company), but the EITF has concluded that the fair value of the stock compensation (as measured on the *grant date*) is recognized as a *dividend* to the controlling company with an offsetting contribution to capital (EITF Issue No. 00-23, Issue 21).

## Tracking Stock

Interpretation 44 does not provide guidance in regard to how "tracking stock" is to be accounted for under Opinion 25, but the EITF has concluded that if the tracking stock is "substantive," the stock compensation should be accounted for in the separate subsidiary and consolidated financial statements under Opinion 25 and not Statement 123 (EITF Issue No. 00-23, Issue 28(a)).

Tracking stock is considered for legal and accounting purposes to be equity of the parent company, and not equity of the unit or subsidiary to which the stock tracks.

A tracking stock is considered substantive if it is publicly traded (other criteria may also lead to the determination that the tracking stock is substantive).

If the tracking stock is not substantive, the award should be accounted for as a cash-based or formula arrangement in both the separate subsidiary and consolidated financial statements.

## LLC Profits Interest Awards

Interpretation 44 does not provide guidance in regard to how to account for a profits interest in an LLC, but the EITF has concluded that the grantee of a profits interest award in an LLC should be considered an employee under Opinion 25 if the grantee qualifies as a common law employee; the fact that the LLC does not classify the grantee as an employee for payroll tax purposes is not relevant (EITF Issue No. 00-23, Issue 40(a)).

The EITF also has concluded that if a grantee of a profits interest award is considered to be an employee for purposes of applying Opinion 25, the award should be accounted for as fixed or variable based on its substance taking into consideration all relevant facts and circumstances, including the investment required, liquidation or prepayment provisions, and provisions for the realization of value (EITF Issue No. 00-23, Issue 40(b)).

### Application of Opinion 25

The application of Opinion 25 in consolidated and separate company financial statements under various grantor/employee scenarios is summarized in table 3-1.

## Changes in Status

### In General

There may be an accounting consequence for a grantor company if an individual with outstanding stock options or awards changes status to or from that of an employee, and the individual *continues to provide services* to the grantor company; a change in status can occur directly, such as when an employee transfers to a nonconsolidated company (such as a joint venture), or indirectly, such as when an employee works for a consolidated subsidiary that is subsequently deconsolidated.

### If a Change in Status Occurs

If a change in status occurs, the grantor company must "remeasure" compensation cost as if outstanding stock options or awards are newly granted as of the date of change in status, using the intrinsic value method under Opinion 25 if the individual changes status to an employee, or the fair value method under Statement 123 if the individual changes status to a nonemployee.

**Table 3-1**

| Stock Compensation Granted By | Stock Compensation Granted to Employees of: | | |
| --- | --- | --- | --- |
| | Parent Company | Consolidated Subsidiary | Nonconsolidated Subsidiary |
| *Consolidated Financial Statements:* | | | |
| — Parent company | **Opinion 25 applies** | **Opinion 25 applies** | Opinion 25 does not apply |
| — Consolidated subsidiary | **Opinion 25 applies** | **Opinion 25 applies** | Opinion 25 does not apply |
| *Subsidiary Financial Statements:* | | | |
| — Parent company | Not applicable | **Opinion 25 applies** | Opinion 25 does not apply |
| — Consolidated subsidiary | Opinion 25 does not apply | Opinion 25 does not apply* | Opinion 25 does not apply |
| — Nonconsolidated subsidiary | Opinion 25 does not apply | Opinion 25 does not apply | Opinion 25 does not apply* |

* Opinion 25 does apply if the stock compensation is granted by a subsidiary to employees of that same subsidiary.

## If Outstanding Awards Are Not Modified

If the original terms of outstanding stock options or awards are not modified coincident with a change in status (that is, there is no change to the exercise period, vesting provisions, exercise price, or number of shares), only that portion of newly measured compensation cost attributable to the *remaining* vesting period is recognized over the remaining vesting period of the awards (if 40% of the vesting period has expired, for example, only the remaining 60% of newly measured compensation cost is recognized over the remaining vesting period of the award); compensation cost (if any) recognized prior to the change in status under the prior method of accounting is *not* reversed, unless the award is subsequently forfeited.

There is no accounting consequence (that is, there is no remeasurement of compensation cost) if, as of the change in status, the outstanding stock options or awards are fully vested and not otherwise modified coincident with the change.

## If Outstanding Awards Are Modified to Continue or Accelerate Vesting

If the original terms of outstanding stock options or awards provide for the forfeiture of the awards upon a change in status and the awards are modified coincident with the change to continue or accelerate vesting, the awards are deemed to be "reinstated," and the *total amount* of newly measured compensation cost is fully recognized either immediately (if the awards become fully vested as a result of the modification) or over the remaining vesting period of the award; compensation cost (if any) recognized prior to the change in status under the prior method of accounting is fully reversed at the change in status date.

## If Outstanding Awards Are Modified Other Than to Continue or Accelerate Vesting

Interpretation 44 does not provide guidance in situations where the original terms of outstanding stock options or awards provide that the awards are to be *retained* upon a change in status (that is, the awards are not forfeited), but the awards are nevertheless modified other than to continue or accelerate vesting coincident with the change (that is, there is a change to the exercise period, exercise price, or number of shares); the EITF has concluded, however, that (1) compensation cost is remeasured at the modification date using the method of accounting appropriate for the grantee's status *before* the change, and is recognized at the modification date only for the portion of newly measured compensation cost attributable to the *expired* vesting period of the award (in addition, variable award accounting is required prospectively for this portion of the award if the modification is a repricing that occurs concurrent with a change in status from employee to nonemployee), and (2) compensation cost is also remeasured at the modification date using the method of accounting appropriate for the grantee's status *after* the change (as if the award is newly granted), and is recognized over the remaining vesting period only for the portion of newly measured compensation cost attributable to the *remaining* vesting period of the award (EITF Issue No. 00-23, Issues 18, 19, and 20).

## Exception for Spinoff Transactions

If an individual changes status from an employee to a nonemployee as a result of a spinoff transaction (that is, a pro rata distribution to company shareholders of shares of a subsidiary such that the company no longer consolidates the former subsidiary), the grantor company does *not* change its method of accounting from Opinion 25 to the fair value method for stock options or awards previously granted to the individual as an employee; thus, there is no accounting consequence to the grantor company provided the requirements for "equity restructurings" (discussed below) are satisfied.

The exception applies solely to changes in status as a result of a spinoff transaction, and only for stock options or awards granted prior to the change in status (including adjustments to those awards coincident with the spinoff).

The exception does not apply to changes in status as a result of an exchange transaction such as a sale, public offering, split-off, or split-up, or to stock options or awards granted after the spinoff transaction (that is, the fair value method applies).

### Consequence of a Change in Status

The accounting consequences of a change in status under various employment/modification scenarios are summarized in table 3-2.

# Noncompensatory Plans

Employee stock purchase plans meeting the criteria under Section 423 of the Internal Revenue Code are deemed to be "noncompensatory" under Opinion 25, and thus do not result in compensation cost to the grantor company; permissible provisions include (1) purchase discounts of up to 15% of the stock price at grant and (2) purchase prices based on the *lesser of* the stock price on the date of grant or the date of purchase, i.e., "look-back" purchase prices.

The EITF has concluded that compensatory plan accounting is required under Opinion 25 for any employee stock purchase plan with purchase discount or exercise period provisions that exceed Internal Revenue Code Section 423 limits, regardless of whether the plan is deemed noncompensatory outside the United States; further, variable award accounting is required for such plans if the grantee can elect to cancel (and forfeit) one purchase contract and within six months enter into a new contract offered by the employer at a lower exercise price (that is, the transaction is viewed as a repricing) (EITF Issue No. 00-23, Issues 42(a), 42(b), and 42(c)).

# Modifications in General

### In General

Modifications are relevant only in regard to otherwise fixed stock options or awards because the final measure of compensation cost for variable awards does not occur until the awards are vested (or in some cases exercised), regardless of whether the awards are modified or not; certain modifications to the original terms of otherwise fixed stock options or awards may result in either (1) a new measurement date or (2) potentially more punitive variable award accounting.

## Table 3-2

| Scenario | Accounting Consequence at Change in Status if Original Terms of Award Provide for:* | | |
| --- | --- | --- | --- |
| | Accelerated Vesting | Continued Vesting | Award Forfeiture |
| *Scenario 1*<br><br>Grantee does not continue to provide services.<br><br>Awards are not modified at the change in status. | **No accounting consequence** | **No accounting consequence** | Compensation cost (if any) recognized prior to the change in status is reversed in full in the period of forfeiture. |
| *Scenario 2*<br><br>Grantee does not continue to provide services.<br><br>Awards are modified to accelerate vesting at the change in status (including the use of "discretion" to accelerate vesting). | Not Applicable | Compensation cost is remeasured at the modification date using the method of accounting appropriate for the grantee's status *prior* to the change.<br><br>Any remaining or newly measured compensation cost is recognized in full (if required in accordance with the appropriate method of accounting) at the change in status because no remaining services are required by the grantee, i.e., the award is substantively vested. | Compensation cost is remeasured at the modification date using the method of accounting appropriate for the grantee's status *prior* to the change.<br><br>Any remaining or newly measured compensation cost is recognized in full at the change in status because no remaining services are required by the grantee, i.e., the award is substantively vested. |

*A change in grantee status refers to a *substantive* change from employee status to nonemployee status (or vice versa); "temporary" changes in status that are remedied are generally regarded as *not* substantive. The appropriate method of accounting is the "intrinsic value" method under APB Opinion No. 25 for employees, and the "fair value" method under FASB Statement No. 123 for nonemployees.

**Table 3-2 (continued)**

| Scenario | Accounting Consequence at Change in Status if Original Terms of Award Provide for:* | | |
| --- | --- | --- | --- |
| | Accelerated Vesting | Continued Vesting | Award Forfeiture |
| *Scenario 3*<br>Grantee does not continue to provide services.<br><br>Awards are modified other than to accelerate vesting at the change in status. | Compensation cost is remeasured at the modification date using the method of accounting appropriate for the grantee's status *prior* to the change.<br><br>Any remaining or newly measured compensation cost is recognized in full at the change in status because no remaining services are required by the grantee, i.e., the award is substantively vested; in addition, variable award accounting is required prospectively if the modification is a repricing that occurs concurrent with a change in status from employee to nonemployee | Compensation cost is remeasured at the modification date using the method of accounting appropriate for the grantee's status *prior* to the change.<br><br>Any remaining or newly measured compensation cost is recognized in full at the change in status because no remaining services are required by the grantee, i.e., the award is substantively vested; in addition, variable award accounting is required prospectively if the modification is a repricing that occurs concurrent with a change in status from employee to nonemployee. | Compensation cost (if any) recognized prior to the change in status is reversed in full in the period of forfeiture. |

* A change in grantee status refers to a *substantive* change from employee status to nonemployee status (or vice versa); "temporary" changes in status that are remedied are generally regarded as *not* substantive. The appropriate method of accounting is the "intrinsic value" method under APB Opinion No. 25 for employees, and the "fair value" method under FASB Statement No. 123 for nonemployees.

## Table 3-2 (continued)

| Scenario | Accounting Consequence at Change in Status if Original Terms of Award Provide for:* | | |
| --- | --- | --- | --- |
| | Accelerated Vesting | Continued Vesting | Award Forfeiture |
| *Scenario 4*<br><br>Grantee continues to provide services.<br><br>Awards are not modified at the change in status. | **No accounting consequence** | Compensation cost is remeasured at the change in status date using the method of accounting appropriate for the grantee's status *after* the change (as if the award is newly granted), and is recognized over the remaining vesting period only for the portion of newly measured compensation cost attributable to the *remaining* vesting period of the award.<br><br>No adjustment is made to compensation cost (if any) recognized prior to the change in status under the prior method of accounting, unless the grantee fails to fulfill an obligation. | Compensation cost (if any) recognized prior to the change in status is reversed in full in the period of forfeiture. |

*A change in grantee status refers to a *substantive* change from employee status to nonemployee status (or vice versa); "temporary" changes in status that are remedied are generally regarded as *not* substantive. The appropriate method of accounting is the "intrinsic value" method under APB Opinion No. 25 for employees, and the "fair value" method under FASB Statement No. 123 for nonemployees.

## Table 3-2 (continued)

| | Accounting Consequence at Change in Status if Original Terms of Award Provide for:* | | |
|---|---|---|---|
| Scenario | Accelerated Vesting | Continued Vesting | Award Forfeiture |
| *Scenario 5*<br>Grantee continues to provide services.<br><br>Awards are modified to accelerate vesting at the change in status (including the use of "discretion" to accelerate vesting). | Not Applicable | Compensation cost is remeasured at the modification date using the method of accounting appropriate for the grantee's status *prior* to the change.<br><br>Any remaining or newly measured compensation cost is recognized in full (if required in accordance with the appropriate method of accounting) at the change in status because no remaining services are required by the grantee, i.e., the award is substantively vested. | Compensation cost is remeasured at the modification date using the method of accounting appropriate for the grantee's status *after* the change (as if the award is newly granted), and is recognized in full at the change in status if no remaining services are required by the grantee or over the remaining vesting (service) period of the award.<br><br>Compensation cost (if any) recognized prior to the modification date (under the prior method of accounting) is reversed in full at the change in status, i.e., the original award is deemed to be forfeited. |

*A change in grantee status refers to a *substantive* change from employee status to nonemployee status (or vice versa); "temporary" changes in status that are remedied are generally regarded as *not* substantive. The appropriate method of accounting is the "intrinsic value" method under APB Opinion No. 25 for employees, and the "fair value" method under FASB Statement No. 123 for nonemployees.

**Table 3-2 (continued)**

| Scenario | Accounting Consequence at Change in Status if Original Terms of Award Provide for:* | | |
|---|---|---|---|
| | Accelerated Vesting | Continued Vesting | Award Forfeiture |
| *Scenario 6*<br>Grantee continues to provide services. Awards are modified other than to accelerate vesting at the change in status. | Compensation cost is remeasured at the modification date using the method of accounting appropriate for the grantee's status *prior* to the change.<br><br>Any remaining or newly measured compensation cost is recognized in full at the change in status because no remaining services are required by the grantee, i.e., the award is substantively vested; in addition, variable award accounting is required prospectively if the modification is a repricing that occurs concurrent with a change in status from employee to nonemployee. | Compensation cost is remeasured at the modification date using the method of accounting appropriate for the grantee's status *prior* to the change, and is recognized at the modification date only for the portion of newly measured compensation cost attributable to the *expired* vesting period of the award; in addition, variable award accounting is required prospectively for this portion of the award if the modification is a repricing that occurs concurrent with a change in status from employee to nonemployee.<br><br>Compensation cost is also remeasured at the modification date using the method of accounting appropriate for the grantee's status *after* the change (as if the award is newly granted), and is recognized over the remaining vesting period only for the portion of newly measured compensation cost attributable to the *remaining* vesting period of the award. | Compensation cost (if any) recognized prior to the change in status is reversed in full in the period of forfeiture. |
| *Scenario 7*<br>Grantee changes status as result of a spinoff. | **No accounting consequence, provided the awards are modified in accordance with guidance for equity restructurings.** | **No accounting consequence, provided the awards are modified in accordance with guidance for equity restructurings.** | Compensation cost (if any) recognized prior to the change in status is reversed in full in the period of forfeiture. |

*A change in grantee status refers to a *substantive* change from employee status to nonemployee status (or vice versa); "temporary" changes in status that are remedied are generally regarded as *not* substantive. The appropriate method of accounting is the "intrinsic value" method under APB Opinion No. 25 for employees, and the "fair value" method under FASB Statement No. 123 for nonemployees.

## Modifications That Result in a New Measurement Date

A new measurement date is required for otherwise fixed stock options or awards that are modified to either (1) extend the maximum contractual exercise period or the post-termination exercise period of a stock option or (2) renew a stock option or award through the acceleration or continuation of vesting; if a new measurement date is required, compensation cost is remeasured (as if the award is newly granted) based on the award's intrinsic value as of the modification date.

## Modifications That Result in Variable Award Accounting

Variable award accounting is required for otherwise fixed stock options or awards that are modified to directly or indirectly change either (1) the exercise or purchase price of the award through a "repricing" or a "cancellation and replacement" of the award or (2) the number of shares underlying the award through the addition of a "reload" feature; if variable award accounting is required, compensation cost is a measured each period (based on the stock price at the end of each period) until the modified award is exercised, is forfeited, or expires unexercised.

## Modifications That Result in No Accounting Consequence

Neither a new measurement date nor variable award accounting is apparently required for otherwise fixed stock options or awards that are modified other than to (1) extend the maximum contractual or post-termination exercise period, (2) provide for an acceleration or continuation of vesting, or (3) change the exercise price or the number of shares underlying the award; examples of permissible modifications include the addition of option gain deferral provisions, limited transferability provisions, and stock-for-stock exercise and minimum statutory stock-for-tax withholding provisions.

The EITF has concluded that a transferability provision (either pursuant to the original terms of the award or through a subsequent modification of the award) does not result in an accounting consequence, unless all relevant facts and circumstances indicate (1) the subsequent transfer results in a reacquisition of the award by the employer (for example, the transfer results in the payment of cash or other consideration by the employer to reacquire the award) or (2) the employer facilitates the transfer to circumvent existing accounting rules, as would be the case if the employer uses the employee as a conduit to transfer the award to a nonemployee service provider (thereby avoiding the accounting requirements of Statement 123 and EITF Issue No. 96-18) (EITF Issue No. 00-23, Issue 46).

# Extending the Exercise Period of a Stock Option

## In General

A new measurement date is required for otherwise fixed stock options that are modified to *extend* either the maximum contractual exercise period or the post-termination exercise period of the award; modifications that *reduce* the exercise period of the award presumably do not result in a new measurement date (because the exercise period is not extended) but could result in an effective cancellation of the award for purposes of the cancellation and replacement provisions discussed below.

An indirect extension of the maximum contractual or post-termination exercise period may occur if a stock option is modified to permit exercise using a nonrecourse note that matures after the original exercise period of the award.

### Extension of Maximum Contractual Exercise Period

A modification that extends the maximum contractual exercise period of a stock option (including a modification contingent upon a future separation from employment) results in a new measurement date as of the modification date, with compensation cost equal to the excess of the award's intrinsic value as of the modification date over the award's original intrinsic value (if any); compensation cost is recognized over the remaining vesting period (or recognized immediately if the award is fully vested as of the modification date) *for any individual who could benefit from the modification.*

### Extension of Post-Termination Exercise Period

A modification that extends the exercise period of a stock option upon separation from employment (but not beyond the maximum contractual exercise period) results in a new measurement date as of the modification date, with compensation cost equal to the excess of the award's intrinsic value as of the modification date over the award's original intrinsic value (if any); compensation cost is recognized (either immediately or over the remaining vesting period, if any) *only if and when* a separation event occurs and the exercise period is extended.

Companies are to estimate as of the modification date (to the extent possible) the likelihood of an extension and begin to recognize compensation cost based on those estimates, with adjustments in later periods to the extent actual experience differs from prior estimates.

## Acceleration or Continuation of Vesting

### In General

A new measurement date is required for otherwise fixed stock options or awards that are modified to *accelerate or continue* the vesting period of the award; modifications that *extend* the vesting period of the award presumably do not result in a new measurement date (because there is no renewal of the award), but could result in an effective cancellation of the award for purposes of the cancellation and replacement provisions discussed below.

A new measurement date is *not* required for otherwise fixed stock options or awards if vesting is accelerated pursuant to the *original terms* of the award.

### Using Discretion or Modifying an Award to Accelerate or Continue Vesting

Using discretion or modifying the original terms of an otherwise fixed stock option or award to accelerate or continue vesting (whether unconditionally or upon the occurrence of a specified future event) results in a new measurement date as of the date discretion is used or the award is modified, with compensation cost equal to the excess of the award's intrinsic value as of the modification date over the award's original intrinsic value (if any); compensation cost is recognized *only if and when* an individual becomes vested in an award that, pursuant to the original terms of the award, would have been forfeited absent the acceleration or continuation.

Compensation cost is not recognized if the employee continues to provide services and eventually becomes vested pursuant to the original vesting provisions of the award.

Companies are to estimate as of the modification date (to the extent possible) the likelihood of an acceleration or continuation and begin to recognize compensation cost based on those estimates, with adjustments in later periods to the extent actual experience differs from prior estimates.

## Early Exercise of Nonvested Stock Options

Interpretation 44 does not provide guidance in regard to how to account for the "early exercise" of a stock option if the employer has a contingent repurchase or "call" right until the award is vested with a strike price equal to the *lesser of* fair value of the stock at the call date or the original exercise price paid by the employee (sometimes referred to as a "California Style" stock option), but the EITF has concluded that the contingent call right is in substance a forfeiture provision that preserves the original vesting schedule of the award and results in no adverse accounting consequences for an otherwise fixed stock option, provided the call right (1) expires at the end of the original vesting period of the award, (2) becomes exercisable only if a termination event occurs that would have caused the award to be forfeited, and (3) is priced at the *lower of* the employee's exercise price or the fair value of the stock on the date the call is exercised; an acceleration of vesting occurs if the employee terminates employment prior to vesting and the employer fails to exercise the call right (EITF Issue No. 00-23, Issue 33(a)).

In addition, the shares received upon early exercise are not considered "issued" for purposes of computing basic earnings per share (EPS) or determining whether the shares are "mature.

The guidance above applies regardless of whether the early exercise provision is pursuant to the original terms of the stock option or added through a subsequent modification of the award.

The EITF also has concluded that if the strike price for the employer call right is based *solely* on the original exercise price paid by the employee (that is, *not* the lesser of fair value of the stock at the call date or the original exercise price), the early exercise is *not* recognized for accounting purposes; rather, any cash paid for the exercise price is considered a deposit or prepayment of the exercise price that should be recognized by the employer as a liability (EITF Issue No. 00-23, Issue 33(b)).

The stock options should only be accounted for as exercised when the awards become vested and the employer repurchase right lapses; an acceleration of vesting occurs if the employee terminates employment prior to vesting and the employer fails to exercise the call right.

# Stock Option Repricings and Cancellation/Replacement Awards

## In General

Variable award accounting is required for otherwise fixed stock options that are modified to directly or indirectly *reduce* the exercise price of the award; modifications that *increase* the exercise price of the award are not directly addressed by Interpretation 44 but could result in an effective cancellation of the award for purposes of the cancellation and replacement provisions discussed below.

Variable award accounting applies from the date of modification until the date the award is exercised, is forfeited, or expires unexercised.

The EITF has concluded that modifications that increase the exercise price of the award result in either a new measurement date or variable award accounting, depending on all relevant facts and circumstances (EITF Issue No. 00-23, Issue 26).

A new measurement date is required if it is possible to conclude that further changes to the exercise price will not occur in the future, such as when unusual modifications are sometimes made to comply with the regulatory environment.

Variable award accounting is required if there is no practical way to ascertain whether further changes to the exercise price will occur in the future; factors to consider include (1) whether the award has been similarly modified in the past, (2) whether the modification is related to the grantee's job performance, or (3) whether other factors indicate that similar modifications are possible in the future.

The EITF also has concluded that a "settlement" of nonvested stock awards in connection with the grant of new "at-the-money" stock options represents an "upward repricing" that should be evaluated in accordance with the guidance in Issue 26 (EITF Issue No. 00-23, Issue 37(b)).

The EITF also has concluded that the exercise price of a stock option is not fixed (and thus variable award accounting is required) if either (1) the award is modified to add a "short-term inducement" to exercise the stock option (EITF Issue No. 00-23, Issue 30) or (2) the exercise price is denominated in multiple currencies or in a currency other than the currency of the "primary economic environment of either the employer or the employee" (EITF Issue No. 00-23, Issue 31).

## Stock Option Repricings

A "repricing" is a direct or an indirect reduction to the exercise price of a fixed stock option such that the fair value of the exercise price after modification is *less than* the fair value of the exercise price prior to the modification; examples of indirect repricings include modifications that provide for a (1) cash bonus arrangement that is contingent upon option exercise, (2) below-market interest loan to facilitate option exercise, or (3) reduction to the exercise price if a specified future event occurs (such as the attainment of a performance condition).

The FASB staff has concluded that an indirect repricing also occurs if a "new" stock option is granted with a lower exercise and an exercise period that expires upon the earlier of (1) the normal exercise period (10 years) or (2) 30 days after the date at which the company's stock price reaches the exercise price of previously granted "underwater" stock options; an indirect repricing is *not* deemed to occur, however, if the expiration of the exercise period occurs *at least six months after* the stock price test is attained (FASB Staff Announcement Topic No. D-91).

The EITF has concluded that the fact pattern in FASB Staff Announcement Topic No. D-91 should be clarified to provide that variable award accounting is required for stock options that could expire *prior to vesting* because of a truncation provision for reasons other than the grantee's termination of employment (because the number of shares is not fixed); variable award accounting applies until the stock options become vested (EITF Issue No. 00-23, Issue 45).

## Cancellation and Replacement Awards

An actual or "effective" cancellation of a stock option combined with the "replacement" of a new stock option at a lower exercise price during a six-month "look-back look-forward" period is deemed to be a reduction in exercise price that requires variable award accounting for the replacement award from the date of cancellation (or the date of replacement, if later) until the date the replacement award is exercised, is forfeited, or expires unexercised.

The settlement of a stock option for cash or other consideration is also considered a cancellation that can be combined with a replacement award.

## Effective Cancellations

An effective cancellation is deemed to occur if an outstanding stock option is modified to "reduce or eliminate the likelihood of exercise," including modifications that (1) reduce the exercise period, (2) extend the vesting period, (3) increase the exercise price, or (4) reduce the number of shares of the award; an effective cancellation is also deemed to occur if, at the time the replacement award is granted, an agreement exists (in any form) to cancel or settle an outstanding stock option at a specified future date (including a "tandem" award, whereby the exercise of one award cancels the other, and vice versa).

The EITF has concluded that a "statutory transfer" of an employer's United Kingdom employment tax liability through a modification to an otherwise fixed award is *not* deemed to be an effective cancellation, because the modification is not expected to reduce the likelihood of exercise (EITF Issue No. 00-23, Issue 17).

The EITF also has concluded that whether reducing (or "truncating") the exercise period of stock options actually reduces or eliminates the likelihood of exercise depends on whether the stock options are in-the-money or underwater (EITF Issue No. 00-23, Issue 39(g)).

The truncation of in-the-money stock options generally should *not* reduce the likelihood of exercise (in fact, the truncation may actually *increase* the likelihood of exercise), and thus should not result in an effective cancellation of the options; judgment should be applied in evaluating relevant facts and circumstances when making this determination.

The truncation of underwater stock options does reduce the likelihood of exercise, however, resulting in an effective cancellation and a window of evaluation for identifying replacement awards that begins six months before the announcement of the truncation (or six months before the event triggering the truncation if the truncation is pursuant to the embedded terms of the option) and ending six months after the options expire; refer to discussion of the look-back look-forward period below.

The EITF also has concluded that, if existing stock options are canceled without the company providing substantial consideration in exchange for the cancellation, a rebuttable presumption exists that the cancellation is linked to a previous stock option with a lower exercise price; thus, if the presumption is not overcome, variable award accounting is required for the previous stock option even if granted more than six months before the cancellation (the six-month safe harbor is not relevant if there is evidence of an implied agreement at grant to cancel a stock option in the future) (EITF Issue 00-23, Issue 39(f)).

## Look-Back Look-Forward Period

In identifying potential replacement awards with a lower exercise price, companies are to first "look back" to the period that begins six months before the actual or effective cancellation date (or the grant date of the canceled stock option, if more recent), first identifying awards with grant dates in the closest proximity to the cancellation date; if the number of canceled stock options exceeds the number of replacement awards identified in the look-back period, companies are to then "look forward" to the period that ends six months after the actual or effective cancellation date (again, first identifying awards with grant dates in the closest proximity to the cancellation date).

If the number of canceled stock options exceeds the number of replacement awards identified in the look-back look-forward period, no further identification of potential replacement awards is required.

If the number of stock options granted during the look-back look-forward period exceeds the number of canceled stock options, the excess number of shares granted are not considered to be replacement awards (that is, variable award accounting is not required for stock options granted during the look-back look-forward period in excess of the number of canceled stock options).

If, at the time a stock option is canceled, there exists any oral or written agreement or implied promise to compensate the employee for stock price increases until a new stock option is granted, the look-forward period becomes irrelevant and the new stock option is deemed to be a replacement award subject to variable award accounting, even if granted outside the look-forward period; the EITF has concluded that the grant of a new "in-the-money" stock option more than six months after cancellation of an underwater stock option results in variable award accounting for the new stock option, unless all relevant facts and circumstances indicate the new stock option was not "intended to compensate the grantee for stock price increases after cancellation of the old stock option" (EITF Issue No. 00-23, Issue 24); the EITF also has concluded that the grant of new "at-the-money" stock options more than six months after cancellation of underwater stock options results in variable award accounting for the new stock options if the number of new stock options [presumably] exceeds the number of canceled stock options and is based on a formula that is either directly or indirectly linked to changes in the market price of the underlying stock (because the formula is presumably intended to compensate the grantee for stock price increases) (EITF Issue No. 00-23, Issue 39(d)).

If the canceled stock option was previously accounted for as a variable award because of a prior direct or indirect reduction in exercise price, *any* stock option granted during the look-back look-forward period is eligible to be a replacement award subject to variable award accounting (not just stock options with a lower exercise price).

## Employer Offers to Cancel and Replace

Interpretation 44 does not provide guidance in regard to an employer's "offer" to cancel existing stock options and (upon acceptance of the offer) grant new replacement awards, but the EITF has concluded the following:

- An employer's offer to grant new replacement stock options with a lower exercise price *within six months of* the cancellation date of the existing stock options (that is, an offer to "reprice" the existing stock options) results in variable award accounting for *all* existing stock options subject to the offer; variable award accounting commences when the offer is made, and for the stock options that are retained because the offer is declined, continues until the options are exercised, are forfeited, or expire unexercised (EITF Issue No. 00-23, Issue 36(a)).

- If existing stock options are subject to variable award accounting because of an employer's offer to reprice, upon acceptance of the offer and cancellation of the existing stock options, *any* new stock options granted during the six-month look-back look-forward period are eligible to be replacement awards subject to variable award accounting treatment (not just new stock options with a *lower* exercise price) (EITF Issue No. 00-23, Issue 36(b)).

- An employer's offer to grant new replacement stock options with an "at-the-money" exercise price *more than six months after* the cancellation of the existing stock options results in no adverse accounting consequences for existing stock options subject to the offer, provided the six-month "safe harbor" provisions of Interpretation 44 are satisfied (in substance, the employer has only offered to "cancel" the existing stock options, not "reprice" the options) (EITF Issue No. 00-23, Issue 36(c)).

- If the terms of the offer call for replacement in the form of *restricted stock*, all existing stock options subject to the offer become subject to variable award accounting, even if the offer calls for replacement more than six months after cancellation; the rationale is that an offer to grant restricted stock more than six months after cancellation is in substance the same as an offer to grant restricted stock immediately upon cancellation (because restricted stock protects the grantee from stock price increases subsequent to cancellation, regardless of when granted) (EITF Issue No. 00-23, Issues 39(a) and 39(b)).

- The look-back look-forward period for purposes of identifying replacement awards in connection with a cancellation/replacement

offer begins six months prior to commencement of the offer period
(that is, the date the offer is communicated to employees), continues *through* the offer period, and ends six months after the existing
stock options are legally canceled (that is, the date that all legal and
regulatory requirements for cancellation are met, such as the date
an election to cancel can no longer be revoked); thus, the effect of a
lengthy offer period or the existence of multiple offers is to *lengthen*
the six-month look-back look-forward period for purposes of identifying replacement awards (EITF Issue No. 00-23, Issues 36(d) and
36(e)).

- If the terms of a cancellation offer provide for the *reinstatement* of
previously canceled stock options or the *acceleration* of the grant of
new replacement awards during the six-month safe harbor period
upon the occurrence of certain events (such as death, involuntary
termination, or change-in-control), the cancellation date and related
commencement of the six-month look-forward period cannot occur
until the canceled stock options can no longer be reinstated or the
grant of new replacement awards can no longer be accelerated; thus,
the cancellation date is generally the same date the new replacement
awards are granted, resulting in a violation of the six-month safe
harbor and variable award accounting for all existing stock options
subject to the offer and all new replacement stock options (EITF Issue No. 00-23, Issue 39(c)).

- If the terms of a cancellation offer provide for a portion of the new
replacement stock options to be granted immediately upon cancellation (to protect the grantee against stock price increases during
the six-month safe harbor) and a portion to be granted more than
six months after cancellation (to avoid variable award accounting
for that portion of the grant), variable award accounting is required
for the initial replacement stock options granted immediately upon
cancellation because the six-month safe harbor is violated; variable
award accounting is also required for a portion of the remaining
replacement stock options granted more than six months after cancellation if the exercise period for the initial replacement stock options expires *within* six months of the grant of the remaining stock
options, consistent with the indirect repricing guidance in FASB Staff

Announcement Topic No. D-91; the number of remaining replacement stock options subject to variable award accounting is equal to the number of initial stock options granted (fixed award accounting applies to any remaining replacement stock options in excess of the number of initial replacement stock options granted); variable award accounting is *not* required for the remaining replacement stock options granted more than six months after cancellation if either (1) the exercise period for the initial replacement stock options expires *more than six months after* the grant of the remaining replacement stock options or (2) the initial stock options are granted in the form of restricted stock, regardless of when granted (because restricted stock is always viewed as a "replacement award," rather than as "consideration for stock price increases" during the six-month safe harbor) (EITF Issue No. 00-23, Issue 39(e)).

### Cancellation and Replacement With Stock

If a fixed or variable stock option is canceled and replaced with a stock award that requires no exercise or purchase price from the employee (such as the grant of restricted stock), a new measurement date is required with respect to the stock award resulting in compensation cost equal to the award's intrinsic value at the date of grant.

Variable award accounting is not required for the new stock award because future reductions in the exercise price are not possible.

However, any shares canceled in excess of the number of new stock awards granted can be combined with other replacement awards (that are subject to variable award accounting) during the look-back look-forward period.

# Equity Restructurings

## In General

There is no accounting consequence for otherwise fixed stock options or awards that are modified (regardless of whether the modification is pursuant to the original terms of the award or not) to adjust the exercise price and/or number of shares coincident with an "equity restructuring" (defined as a "nonreciprocal" transaction such as a stock dividend, spinoff, stock split, rights offering, or large nonrecurring dividend that causes a company's stock price to decrease), provided (1) the aggregate intrinsic value of the award is not *increased*, and (2) the ratio of exercise price to market price per share is not *reduced*.

The above criteria are deemed satisfied even if stock options of the divested company are "stapled to" or "blended with" stock options of the divesting company. If the above criteria are not met, variable award accounting applies from the date of modification until the date the award is exercised or forfeited, or expires. If the above criteria are met but the awards are otherwise modified to extend the exercise period or accelerate vesting, a new measurement date is required pursuant to the guidance for extensions and accelerations (discussed above); cash or other consideration paid to restore an employee's economic position is recognized as compensation cost.

Interpretation 44 does not provide guidance in regard to how to adjust outstanding stock options or awards that have *negative* intrinsic value at the time of restructuring, but the EITF has concluded the following (EITF Issue No 00-23, Issue 49):

- There is no accounting consequence provided (1) the aggregate negative intrinsic value is not *reduced* and (2) the ratio of exercise price to market price per share is not *reduced*.

- If the second requirement is satisfied but the aggregate negative intrinsic value is reduced (that is, the first requirement is not satisfied), the exchange is accounted for as the grant of a new award (the number of additional stock options that would have been issued to maintain the same aggregate negative intrinsic value), and a deemed cancellation of those additional awards that would be subject to the look-back look-forward cancellation and replacement guidance discussed above.

- If the second requirement is *not* satisfied, variable award accounting is required for the entire exchanged award.

## "Reciprocal" Equity Restructurings

Interpretation 44 does not provide guidance in regard to how companies are to account for outstanding stock options or awards that are exchanged in connection with a transaction that is *not* a nonreciprocal equity restructuring (such as the exchange of parent-company stock options for subsidiary-company stock options in an initial public offering or the conversion of one class of parent-company tracking stock into another class of tracking or common stock), but the EITF has concluded that the exchange results in a new measurement date if the above criteria *are* met and in variable award accounting if the criteria are *not* met (EITF Issue No. 00-23, Issues 1, 28(b), and 41); if the exchange involves subsidiary-company stock options or awards that were outstanding when the parent company *first gained control* of the subsidiary, the exchange is accounted for by the purchase method rather than as a modification (that is, the fair value of exchanged parent-company stock options or awards is included as part of the purchase consideration for the subsidiary) (EITF Issue No. 00-23, Issue 12).

## Failure to Adjust Awards

Interpretation 44 also does not provide guidance in regard to the accounting consequence of a company's *failure* to adjust outstanding stock options or awards in connection with an equity restructuring, but the EITF has concluded the following (EITF Issue No. 00-23, Issue 43):

- If the embedded terms of stock options or awards *require* equitable adjustments in connection with an equity restructuring but the company nevertheless *fails to do so*, the accounting consequence of such failure is a deemed modification resulting in either (1) a repricing requiring variable award accounting if the effect is a *reduction* in exercise price or (2) either a new measurement date or variable award accounting (depending on all relevant facts and circumstances consistent with the guidance in EITF Issue No. 00-23, Issue 26) if the effect is an *increase* in exercise price; further, if the failure to adjust awards results in a reduced likelihood of exercise, the awards are deemed to be effectively canceled similar to the guidance in EITF Issue No. 00-23, Issue 39(g).

- If in connection with a stock split, reverse stock split, or stock dividend treated as a stock split, the embedded terms of [presumably underwater] stock options provide for equitable adjustment to the exercise price but *not* the number of shares, any such adjustment is deemed to be a repricing requiring variable award accounting (because the aggregate *negative* intrinsic value is reduced).

• If the embedded terms of stock options or awards are *silent* in regard to equitable adjustments in connection with an equity restructuring (or if adjustments are at the *discretion* of the company), the accounting guidance above applies in event of a stock split, reverse stock split, or stock dividend treated as a stock split; the accounting guidance above also applies in event of a spinoff or large nonrecurring cash dividend unless relevant facts and circumstances provide sufficient evidence of a reason *not* to make equitable adjustments, such as the existence of legal or contractual prohibitions such as debt covenants.

# Reload Stock Options

## In General

Variable award accounting is required for otherwise fixed stock options or awards that are modified to *increase* the number of shares underlying the award; modifications that *reduce* the number of shares underlying the award are not directly addressed by Interpretation 44 but could result in an effective cancellation of the award for purposes of the cancellation and replacement provisions discussed above.

Variable award accounting applies from the date of modification until the date the award is exercised, is forfeited, or expires.

The EITF has concluded that modifications that reduce the number of shares underlying the award result in either a new measurement date or variable award accounting, depending on all relevant facts and circumstances (EITF Issue No. 00-23, Issue 26).

A new measurement date is required if it is possible to conclude that further changes to the number of shares will not occur in the future, such as when unusual modifications are sometimes made to comply with the regulatory environment.

Variable award accounting is required if there is no practical way to ascertain whether further changes to the number of shares will occur in the future; factors to consider include (1) whether the award has been similarly modified in the past, (2) whether the modification is related to the grantee's job performance, or (3) whether other factors indicate that similar modifications are possible in the future.

The EITF also has concluded that the number of shares underlying a stock option is not fixed if the award is modified to add a "short-term inducement" to exercise the stock option (EITF Issue No. 00-23, Issue 30).

## Awards Modified to Add a Reload Feature

Variable award accounting is required for otherwise fixed stock options that are modified to add a reload feature (defined as any feature that provides for the grant of a new stock option upon the *exercise* of the modified stock option), regardless of the method used to determine the exercise price, number of shares, or exercise period of the reload grant; variable award accounting is also required for the reload grant itself, if it too is subject to a reload feature.

## Reload Feature Pursuant to Original Terms of Award

Variable award accounting is not required for an otherwise fixed stock option if the reload feature is pursuant to the *original terms* of the award *and* the requirements of EITF Issue No. 90-7 are satisfied; that is, (1) the reload feature provides for the automatic grant of a new stock option with an exercise price equal to the market price on the reload grant date, and (2) the shares tendered in the reload stock-for-stock exercise are "mature" (that is, owned for at least six months).

The EITF has concluded that variable award accounting is not required if the original terms of an otherwise fixed stock option provide a reload feature for shares used to satisfy minimum statutory tax withholding obligations upon exercise, that is, a "tax reload" feature; further, the shares tendered to satisfy minimum statutory tax withholding obligations need not satisfy the six-month holding period requirement in EITF Issue No. 84-18 (EITF Issue No. 00-23, Issue 47).

# Measuring and Recognizing Compensation Cost

## Measuring Compensation Cost

If an otherwise fixed stock option or award is (1) canceled (other than an effective cancellation discussed above), (2) modified such that a new measurement date or variable award accounting is required, or (3) settled for cash or other consideration within six months after option exercise or share issuance, the final measure of compensation cost is determined as follows:

- *Always* recognize as compensation cost the intrinsic value of the award (if any) as of the award's original measurement date.

- Recognize as *additional* compensation cost the intrinsic value of the modified or newly variable award (or the amount paid to settle the award, less any amount paid by the employee to acquire the shares) that exceeds the *lesser of* (1) the intrinsic value of the award (if any) at the original measurement date or (2) the intrinsic value of the award (if any) immediately prior to the cancellation, modification, or settlement of the award.

- Thus, the final measurement of compensation cost for a typical stock option is equal to the award's intrinsic value as of the modification or settlement date.

## Recognizing Compensation Cost

The final measure of compensation cost calculated above is recognized (1) over the remaining vesting period of the award or (2) immediately if the award is or becomes fully vested as of the date of the cancellation, modification, or settlement of the award.

Compensation cost is reversed only if the award is forfeited because the employee fails to "fulfill an obligation"; this guidance applies even if a nonvested fixed stock option is canceled and not replaced with a new award (EITF Issue No. 00-23, Issue 37(a)).

Compensation cost for newly variable awards is *never* adjusted below the original intrinsic value of the award, unless the award is forfeited because the employee fails to fulfill an obligation.

The EITF has concluded that the accelerated accrual methodology prescribed by FASB Interpretation No. 28 is applicable only to variable awards; compensation cost for fixed awards with pro rata vesting can be recognized either on a pro rata or accelerated basis, so long as the methodology is consistently applied (EITF Issue No. 00-23, Issue 7).

# Share Repurchase Features

## Public Companies

For *public* companies (including "controlled" subsidiaries of public companies), variable award accounting is required for any stock option or award with a repurchase feature between an employee and the grantor company (such as a put, call, or right of first refusal) that is not based on the *fair value* of the stock at the repurchase date, unless the repurchase feature is *not expected to be exercised* (the award is considered an "indexed liability").

Variable award accounting applies until the earlier of expiration or exercise of the repurchase feature.

The SEC staff has concluded that the "rescission" of a previously exercised stock option followed by a reinstatement of the original option is, in essence, an employee put to the company that could be at other than fair value; among other negative accounting consequences, such a transaction results in variable award accounting for the reinstated stock option until the *earlier of* expiration or forfeiture of the reinstated option or the end of the tax year in which the reinstated options are exercised (SEC Staff Announcement Topic No. D-93).

## Nonpublic Companies

For *nonpublic* companies (including nonpublic companies with publicly traded debt), variable award accounting is *not* required for an otherwise fixed award if the repurchase price is based on other than fair value (such as "book value"), provided the employee (1) makes a "substantial investment" in the award (defined as an amount equal to 100% of the stated share repurchase price calculated at the date of grant) and (2) bears the "risks and rewards," of share ownership for a reasonable period of time; if a substantial investment is not made (as is typically the case with the grant of a "plain vanilla" stock option), variable award accounting is required from the date of grant until the date the award is exercised (or purchased) and a substantial investment is made.

The EITF has concluded that fixed award accounting applies (so long as the repurchase price is based on fair value) even if the exercise price of a stock option is based on other than fair value, such as a discount from fair value (EITF Issue No. 00-23, Issue 3).

The EITF also has concluded that share repurchase features based on other than fair value for nonpublic companies may *not* meet the substantial investment criterion (even if the employee invests an amount at least equal to the formula share repurchase price calculated at the date of grant) if the formula results in a *de minimis* employee investment that does not approximate fair value (because the employee does not share in the *risks* of ownership); further, share repurchase features that result in an employee investment of zero *never* meet the substantial investment criterion (EITF Issue No. 00-23, Issue 38).

## Six-Month Holding Period Requirement

Notwithstanding the guidance provided above, variable award accounting is required for otherwise fixed stock options or awards with a share repurchase feature if the shares (1) are *expected to be* repurchased within six months after option exercise or share issuance, (2) *can be* repurchased within six months at the volition of the employee, or (3) for public companies, can be repurchased at any time (even after six months) for a *premium* that is not fixed and determinable over the then-current stock price.

For public companies, a repurchase price based on a *fixed* premium (at least six months after option exercise or share issuance) results in additional compensation cost in an amount equal to the premium.

If shares that were not expected to be repurchased within six months after option exercise or share issuance are in fact repurchased, the transaction is treated as a cash settlement of the award (discussed above).

The EITF has provided complex guidance to help companies determine when an employer call right is "expected to" be exercised and when an employee put right "can be" exercised (EITF Issue No. 00-23, Issues 23(a), 23(b), 23(c), and 23(d)).

Essentially, all employer call rights are presumed to be exercised (and thus variable award accounting is required) unless (1) an employer with an "active" call right (that is, a call right that is not contingent on future events) makes a "stated representation" not to call the shares and that representation is consistent with all "relevant facts and circumstances," or (2) the call right is "contingent" upon an event that is outside the control of the employer and the event is "not expected to occur."

All employee put rights are presumed to be exercised (and thus variable award accounting is required) unless the put right is contingent upon an event that is outside the control of the employee and the event is not expected to occur (there are special rules for put rights at a "premium" to fair value).

The accounting consequences of various employer call and employee put right scenarios are summarized in table 3-3.

# Stock-for-Tax Withholding

## In General

A new measurement date is required for otherwise fixed stock options or awards if shares are withheld upon option exercise or share issuance in excess of the *minimum statutory* federal, state, and payroll tax withholding rates applicable to supplemental income; compensation cost is equal to the award's intrinsic value as of the excess withholding date.

## Variable Award Accounting

Variable award accounting is required for otherwise fixed stock options or awards if (1) the ability to withhold in excess of minimum statutory rates is at the volition of the employee or (2) the grantor company exhibits "a pattern of consistently approving excess withholding transactions."

# Business Combinations

## Pooling of Interests

There is no accounting consequence for otherwise fixed stock options that are exchanged in a pooling-of-interests transaction, provided (1) the aggregate intrinsic value of the stock option is not *increased* and (2) the ratio of exercise price to market price per share is not *reduced;* modifications other than to the exercise price or number of shares of the award are not addressed by Interpretation 44 because such modifications would generally preclude pooling.

The EITF has concluded that the "stock out" of vested and nonvested stock options on a fair value basis results in a new measurement date, with compensation cost equal to the intrinsic value of the new stock awards (EITF Issue No. 00-23, Issue 4).

## Table 3-3

| Scenario | Employer / Employee Share Repurchase Rights | | | | |
| --- | --- | --- | --- | --- | --- |
| | Active Rights, i.e., Not Contingent on Future Events | | Contingent Rights, i.e., Contingent on Future Events | | |
| | | | | Outside Control of Employer or Employee | |
| | Employer Representation Not to Call (consistent with relevant facts and circumstances) | No Employer Representation | Within Control of Employer or Employee | Event Expected to Occur | Event Not Expected to Occur |
| *Repurchase Right at Fair Value Within six months of Option Exercise or Share Issuance (substantial investment has been made for nonpublic company)*: | | | | | |
| — Employer Call Rights | **Fixed Award Accounting** | Variable Award Accounting | Assess Under "Active Rights" | Assess Under "Active Rights" | **Fixed Award Accounting** |
| — Employee Put Rights | Not Relevant | Variable Award Accounting | Variable Award Accounting | Variable Award Accounting | **Fixed Award Accounting** |

\* For all fair value repurchase rights, if the terms of the right do not allow repurchase within six months after option exercise or share issuance, the repurchase right does *not* result in variable award accounting; if variable award accounting is required, it should continue until the *earlier of* (1) when the expectation of repurchase no longer exists, (2) when the call or put right expires or is exercised, or (3) when the shares subject to the call or put right are no longer "immature" (compensation cost recognized while the award was accounted for as a variable award should not be reversed if the award is subsequently accounted for as a fixed award).

## Table 3-3 (continued)

| Scenario | Employer / Employee Share Repurchase Rights | | | | |
|---|---|---|---|---|---|
| | Active Rights, i.e., Not Contingent on Future Events | | Contingent Rights, i.e., Contingent on Future Events | | |
| | Employer Representation Not to Call (consistent with relevant facts and circumstances) | No Employer Representation | Within Control of Employer or Employee | Outside Control of Employer or Employee | |
| | | | | Event Expected to Occur | Event Not Expected to Occur |
| **Repurchase Right at Other Than Fair Value (substantial investment has not been made for nonpublic company)\*\*:** | | | | | |
| — Employer Call Rights | **Fixed Award Accounting (unless call right is at less than fair value)** | Variable Award Accounting | Assess Under "Active Rights" | Assess Under "Active Rights" | **Fixed Award Accounting** |
| — Employee Put Rights | Not Relevant | Variable Award Accounting (unless put right is at *fixed premium* over fair value)\*\*\* | Variable Award Accounting (unless put right is at *fixed premium* over fair value)\*\*\* | Variable Award Accounting (unless put right is at *fixed premium* over fair value)\*\*\* | **Fixed Award Accounting** |

\*\*  Whether the repurchase is expected to occur within six months after option exercise or share issuance is not relevant for repurchase rights at other than fair value (unless the repurchase right is at a fixed premium to fair value); if variable award accounting is required, it should continue until the earlier of expiration or exercise of the call or put right (or, for nonpublic companies, six months after the employee makes a substantial investment).

\*\*\*  A put right at a fixed premium over fair value results in either (1) variable award accounting (until the earlier of expiration or exercise of the put right, or six months after option exercise or share issuance) if the put right is exercisable within six months after option exercise or share issuance, or (2) additional compensation cost in an amount equal to the fixed premium (to be recognized over the vesting period) if the put right is *not* exercisable within six months after option exercise or share issuance.

The EITF also has concluded that the "accounting attributes" of stock options or awards exchanged in a pooling-of-interests transaction "carry forward" from the combining company to the issuer; if the combining company accounts for stock options as variable awards because of a prior repricing, for example, the issuer must also account for the exchanged stock options as variable awards (EITF Issue No. 00-23, Issue 8).

## Purchase Business Combinations

The fair value of vested and nonvested stock options or awards exchanged in a purchase business combination is considered part of the purchase proceeds; however, the intrinsic value of nonvested awards attributable to the remaining vesting period of the award (calculated as the intrinsic value of the exchanged award as of the consummation date multiplied by the fraction that is the remaining vesting period divided by the total pre- and post-consummation vesting period) is deducted from the purchase proceeds and allocated to "unearned compensation," which is recognized as compensation cost over the remaining vesting period of the award.

The EITF has concluded that the accounting attributes of stock options or awards exchanged in a purchase business combination do *not* carry forward from the acquiree to the acquirer; the exchanged stock options or awards are accounted for prospectively as "new awards" (EITF Issue 00-23, Issue 8).

The EITF also has provided guidance on several other issues dealing with the accounting for stock options and awards exchanged in a purchase business combination, including:

- The subsequent *repurchase, modification, or forfeiture* of stock options or awards that were previously exchanged in a purchase business combination (EITF Issue No. 00-23, Issues 9, 10, and 11, respectively).

- The appropriate dates that should be used by an acquirer in a purchase business combination to (1) value the stock options or awards exchanged as part of the purchase consideration and (2) measure the intrinsic value (if any) of the exchanged stock options or awards for purposes of allocating a portion of the purchase price to unearned compensation cost (EITF Issue No. 00-23, Issue 13).

- The exchange of acquirer stock options or awards in a purchase business combination for nonvested stock options or awards of an acquiree that are held by *nonemployees* of the acquiree, where the grantees became nonemployees of the acquiree in a prior spinoff transaction (EITF Issue No. 00-23, Issue 14).

- The "income tax benefit" from the exercise of *vested* stock options (including the portion of nonvested stock options attributable to the *expired* vesting period at the consummation date) that were issued in a purchase business combination is recognized as a *reduction* to the purchase price of the acquired business to the extent that the deduction reported for tax purposes does not exceed the fair value of the awards included in the purchase price; the tax benefit of any remaining excess tax deduction is treated as a contribution to capital (EITF No. 00-23, Issues 29(a) and 29(b)).

- Employer payroll taxes associated with the exercise or vesting of stock options or awards that were previously exchanged in a purchase business combination (and that were *vested* at the date the combination was consummated) should be recognized as a liability and corresponding cost on the date of the event triggering the income recognition and payment of tax to the taxing authority (e.g., on the date of exercise for a nonqualified stock option), consistent with the guidance in EITF Issue No. 00-16 (EITF Issue No. 00-23, Issue 32).

## Failure to Assume Awards

Interpretation 44 does not provide guidance in regard to the accounting consequence of a company's *failure* to assume outstanding target company stock options or awards in connection with a purchase business combination, but the EITF has concluded that so long as no legal obligation exists to assume outstanding target company stock options or awards, those awards and any new awards granted by the acquiring company should not be linked for accounting purposes (and any target awards not assumed would not be deemed to be "effectively canceled" for purposes of the cancellation and replacement guidance in Interpretation 44) (EITF Issue No. 00-23, Issue 44).

However, post-acquisition awards should be accounted for as consideration for the purchase business combination if there is evidence of an oral or implied agreement at acquisition to grant new awards to target grantees in exchange for target company stock options or awards after the acquisition (a grant made within one year of acquisition to target employees that differs significantly from the acquiring company's normal grant pattern may provide evidence of such an implied agreement).

## Other Issues

### Shareholder Approval

Stock options or awards that are awarded contingent upon shareholder approval are *not* deemed granted until shareholder approval is actually obtained, unless such approval is perfunctory; thus, a measurement date does not occur *unless and until* shareholder approval is obtained.

The EITF has concluded that the above guidance applies even if the company is not *required* to obtain shareholder approval but nevertheless chooses to do so (EITF Issue No. 00-23, Issue 5).

### Deferred Tax Assets

Deferred tax assets (that is, future tax deductions) for fixed stock options or awards that have intrinsic value at grant are *not* reduced in event of a subsequent decline in stock price (below the stock price at grant).

### Combined Cash and Stock Awards

Variable award accounting is required if the original terms of an otherwise fixed stock option provide for a cash bonus feature that is (1) not fixed and determinable at grant and (2) payable solely upon option exercise; modifications to *add* a cash bonus feature payable solely upon option exercise (regardless of whether the bonus is fixed and determinable or not) are considered to be a repricing of the original award (discussed above).

Compensation cost is determined separately for all other combined cash/stock arrangements; that is, compensation cost is measured separately for the cash and stock components of the award (even if the cash bonus is payable only upon option *vesting*).

The EITF has concluded that cash payments in the form of dividend equivalents that are paid currently or contingent upon vesting do *not* result in variable award accounting for an otherwise fixed award (EITF Issue No. 00-23, Issue 6).

The EITF also has concluded that variable accounting is required if the cash bonus feature is contingent upon the employee's *sale* of stock received from a previous option exercise, because the exercise of the stock option is one of two conditions that must be met in order for the employee to receive the cash bonus (EITF Issue No. 00-23, Issue 27).

The EITF also has provided guidance on several issues dealing with an employee's reimbursement to an employer of certain United Kingdom employment taxes imposed on employers for an employee's option profit at exercise (EITF Issue No. 00-23, Issues 15, 16, and 17).

Interpretation 44 does not provide guidance in regard to how companies are to account for the indirect guarantee of option profits on otherwise fixed stock options by providing for a cash bonus or loan forgiveness if a specified level of intrinsic value is not attained, but the EITF has concluded that the guaranteed minimum gain (generally, the loan or bonus amount) is to be recognized as compensation cost over the applicable service period (with no reversal of cost unless the employee fails to fulfill an obligation); any amount of the bonus *not* paid or loan *not* forgiven (because the specified level of intrinsic value is attained) is treated as a contribution to capital (EITF Issue No. 00-23, Issue 2).

## Stock Option Exercises with Recourse Loans

Interpretation 44 does not provide guidance in regard to whether there are circumstances under which the exercise of a stock option with a full recourse note should *not* be accounted for as an exercise of the option award; the EITF has concluded that the legal form of a recourse loan should be respected (and thus the option exercise should be recognized) unless (1) the employer has legal recourse to the employee's other assets but does not intend to seek repayment beyond the shares issued, (2) the employer has a history of not demanding repayment of loan amounts in excess of the fair value of the shares, (3) the employee does not have sufficient assets or other means (beyond the shares) to justify the recourse nature of the loan, or (4) the employer has accepted a recourse note upon option exercise and subsequently converted the recourse note to a nonrecourse note (EITF Issue No. 00-23, Issue 34).

In addition, all other relevant facts and circumstances should be evaluated when determining whether the note should be accounted for as nonrecourse, including whether the loan is ultimately forgiven or whether a portion of the exercise price can be paid with a nonrecourse loan and the remainder with a recourse loan.

If the facts and circumstances indicate the loan arrangement is non-recourse in substance, the arrangement continues to be accounted for as a stock option in accordance with the guidance in EITF Issue No. 95-16 (that is, the exercise is not recognized for accounting purposes).

The EITF also has concluded that the conversion of a recourse note (that represents consideration for a previous stock compensation transaction) to a nonrecourse note should be accounted for as the repurchase of the shares previously exercised with a recourse note and the simultaneous grant of a new stock option in return for a nonrecourse note, where the repurchase amount is equal to the sum of (1) the then-current principal balance of the recourse note, (2) accrued interest (if any), and (3) the intrinsic value of the new stock option (EITF Issue No. 00-23, Issue 50).

If the repurchase amount exceeds the fair value of the option shares repurchased and the note conversion occurs *more than* six months after option exercise or share issuance, the repurchase is accounted for as a treasury stock transaction, and compensation cost is recognized for the excess of the repurchase amount over the fair value of the shares on the conversion date.

If the repurchase amount exceeds the fair value of the option shares repurchased and the note conversion occurs *within* six months after option exercise or share issuance, the repurchase is accounted for as the acquisition of immature shares, and compensation cost is recognized in accordance with the guidance for award settlements provided in Interpretation 44 (in measuring compensation cost under that guidance, the "amount of cash paid to the employee" is the repurchase amount as defined above).

If the fair value of the option shares repurchased exceeds the repurchase amount (and the employee is not required to pay the difference), the grantor is deemed to have forgiven that portion of the recourse note, and thus all existing and future recourse notes issued in conjunction with option exercises should be accounted for as nonrecourse notes pursuant to the guidance provided in EITF Issue No. 00-23, Issue 34.

The new stock option is accounted for under the nonrecourse note guidance provided in EITF Issue No. 95-16.

The EITF also has concluded that the exercise price of a stock option is not fixed (and thus variable award accounting is required) if the *original terms* of the award provide for exercise with a full recourse note that *may not* bear a market interest rate on the date of exercise (EITF Issue No. 00-23, Issue 25).

Variable award accounting is not required if the interest rate is established *upon exercise* (rather than grant), provided the interest rate is "a market rate based on the rate environment at the date of exercise (based on the credit standing of the grantee)."

## Recourse Loans with Forgiveness Provisions

Interpretation 44 does not provide guidance in regard to how to account for a stock option that is exercised with a recourse note *negotiated at the date of exercise* if the terms of the note or another agreement provide that the note will be forgiven in whole or in part if specified "substantive" performance goals are achieved; the EITF has concluded that provided the performance goals are substantive and the stock option is considered "exercised" for accounting purposes (that is, the loan is not deemed to be "nonrecourse"), variable award accounting is required for the date of exercise (because the exercise price is not fixed for a recourse note arrangement that does not bear market terms); further, any amount of the loan actually forgiven is recognized as additional compensation cost (EITF Issue No. 00-23, Issue 35).

The EITF did not address loan forgiveness arrangements with "nonsubstantive" performance goals, but presumably the option exercise would not be recognized (because the loan is deemed to be nonrecourse), and thus variable award accounting would continue beyond exercise.

The EITF also did not address loan forgiveness arrangements that *are embedded in the terms of an option agreement* rather than issued in conjunction with option exercise or arrangements that are based on *contin-*

*ued service* rather than specified substantive performance goals, but presumably the same variable award accounting would apply because the exercise price is not fixed.

### Broker-Assisted Cashless Exercises

Interpretation 44 does not provide guidance in regard to the accounting consequence of a "cashless exercise" of a stock option effected through a broker, but the EITF has concluded that there is no accounting consequence if the broker is *unrelated* to the grantor, the employee makes a valid exercise of the stock option, and the grantor concludes the employee is legal owner of all option shares (that is, the employee assumes market risk from the moment of exercise until the broker effects the sale on the open market).

If the employee is never the legal owner of the shares, the stock option would be in substance a stock appreciation right (SAR) for which variable accounting would be required (such as when it is illegal for individuals in certain countries to own shares in foreign corporations or for companies in certain countries to allow share ownership by foreign nationals).

The EITF also has concluded that if the broker is a *related party* of the grantor, there is no accounting consequence for a cashless exercise provided (1) the employee takes legal ownership of the option shares as discussed above, (2) the broker-dealer assisting the exercise is a substantive entity with operations that are separate and distinct from those of the grantor (except in circumstances in which the broker-dealer itself is the grantor) and sells the option shares on the open market, and (3) the cashless exercise process is the same whether or not the exercise is being performed for a related entity or an independent entity (EITF Issue No. 00-23, Issue 48).

## Effective Date

### In General

The provisions of Interpretation 44 become effective on July 1, 2000, and (except as noted below) apply to (1) grants of new awards, (2) changes in employee status, (3) modifications to outstanding awards, and (4) exchanges of awards in business combinations that occur on or after that date.

The provisions covering share repurchase features and excess stock-for-tax withholding transactions apply to stock options or awards granted (or new repurchase features added) on or after July 1, 2000.

## Exception for New Grants to Nonemployees

The provisions of Interpretation 44 that exclude stock options or awards granted to nonemployees from the scope of Opinion 25 apply on a prospective basis (beginning July 1, 2000) to new grants to nonemployees that occur *after December 15, 1998.*

## Exception for Stock Option Repricings and Cancellation/Replacement Awards

The provisions of Interpretation 44 dealing modifications to otherwise fixed stock options to directly or indirectly reduce the exercise price apply on a prospective basis (beginning July 1, 2000) to modifications that occur *after December 15, 1998.*

## Exception for Modifications to Add a Reload Feature

The provisions of Interpretation 44 dealing with modifications to otherwise fixed stock options to add a reload feature apply on a prospective basis (beginning July 1, 2000) to modifications that occur *after January 12, 2000.*

## Prospective Application

The provisions of Interpretation 44 apply only on a prospective basis (beginning July 1, 2000) for stock options or awards subject to the "retroactive application dates" discussed above; that is, compensation cost is *not* recognized for amounts attributable to vesting periods or option exercises that occur prior to the July 1, 2000, effective date of Interpretation 44.

The only exception is that, for the presumably few companies that previously accounted for stock compensation granted to nonemployee directors under the fair value provisions of Statement 123, the initial application of Opinion 25 is to be reported as a "cumulative effect of a change in accounting principle."

## EITF Issue No. 00-23

The provisions of EITF Issue No. 00-23 generally apply prospectively beginning after the meeting date on which the specific issue was discussed.

Chapter *4*

# Recent Developments Affecting Opinion 25: EITF 00-23

This chapter provides a detailed analysis and summary of EITF Issue No. 00-23, *Issues Related to the Accounting for Stock Compensation under APB Opinion No. 25 and FASB Interpretation No. 44*. EITF 00-23 was issued to provide further guidance and clarification on the application of Opinion 25 and Interpretation 44. To date, over 50 specific practical issues have been addressed. This chapter discusses those issues, preceded by a key that matches topics with the issues that address them.

## Key to Topics and Relevant Issues

*Award Modifications:* Issues 26, 46

*Broker-Assisted Cashless Exercises:* Issue 48

*Business Combinations:* Issues 4, 8, 9, 10, 11, 13, 14, 29(a), 29(b), 32, 44

*Changes in Status:* Issues 18, 19, 20

*Combined Cash/Stock Awards:* Issues 6, 27, 30

*Equity Restructurings:* Issues 43, 49

*Foreign Currency:* Issue 31

*Guarantee of Option Profits:* Issue 2

*LLC Profits Interest Awards:* Issues 40(a), 40(b)

*Noncompensatory Awards:* Issues 42(a), 42(b), 42(c)

*Option Repricings and Cancellation/Reissuances:* Issues 24, 36(a), 36(b), 36(c), 36(d), 36(e), 37(a), 37(b), 39(a), 39(b), 39(c), 39(d), 39(e), 39(f), 39(g), 45

*Recognition of Compensation Cost:* Issue 7

*Recourse/Nonrecourse Loans:* Issues 25, 34, 35, 50

*Reload Stock Options:* Issue 47

*Scope of Opinion 25:* Issues 21, 22, 51

*Share Repurchase Features:* Issues 3, 23(a), 23(b), 23(c), 23(d), 33(a), 33(b), 38

*Shareholder Approval:* Issue 5

*Stock Option Exchanges:* Issues 1, 12, 41

*Tracking Stock:* Issues 28(a), 28(b)

*United Kingdom National Insurance Taxes:* Issues 15, 16, 17

## Issues

**Note: Issues are in *italic type,* and the EITF consensus appears below each issue in bulleted roman type.**

### Issue 1

*The exchange of outstanding stock options in one member of a consolidated group for stock options in another member of the same group when the exchange does not occur in connection with a "nonreciprocal" equity restructuring (such as a spinoff), e.g., the exchange of parent-company stock options for subsidiary-company stock options (or vice versa) in connection with an initial public offering.*

- The exchange results in a new "measurement date" (and not "variable award" accounting) with respect to the exchanged stock options, provided (1) the aggregate intrinsic value is not *increased* (or negative intrinsic value reduced) and (2) the ratio of exercise price to market price per share is not *reduced*.

- If the above two criteria are not met, the exchange results in variable award accounting, i.e., the exchange is deemed to be an "indirect repricing."

- But refer to Issue 12 if the exchange involves subsidiary-company stock options or awards that were outstanding when the parent company first gained control of the subsidiary

- Also refer to Issues 28(b) and 41 if the exchange involves "tracking stock" or the elimination or exchange of any class of stock.

- The guidance above applies prospectively to modifications to outstanding awards that occur after September 21, 2000 (retroactively to December 15, 1998, if variable award accounting is required).

## Issue 2

*The indirect guarantee of option profits on otherwise fixed stock options by providing a cash bonus or loan forgiveness if a specified level of intrinsic value is not attained within a specified time period.*

- The guaranteed minimum gain (generally the loan or bonus amount) is recognized as compensation cost over the applicable service period, with no reversal of cost unless the employee "fails to fulfill an obligation."

- Any amount of the bonus not paid or loan not forgiven (because the specified level of intrinsic value is attained) is treated as a contribution to capital.

- The related stock option presumably retains its fixed award status.

- The guidance above applies prospectively to new arrangements entered into after September 21, 2000.

## Issue 3

*A nonpublic company grants stock options with a share repurchase feature (that cannot occur within six months of option exercise) based on fair value but an exercise price based on other than fair value, e.g., a discount from fair value.*

- The stock options are subject to "fixed award" accounting (as opposed to variable award accounting), with compensation cost equal to the discount from fair value at grant.
- The guidance above is not subject to a specific prospective application date.

## Issue 4

*The "stock out" of vested and nonvested stock options on a fair value basis in a pooling-of-interests transaction, i.e., the issuer grants stock awards in exchange for outstanding stock options of the combining company on an equivalent fair value basis.*

- The exchange of stock for stock options on a fair value basis in a pooling-of-interests transaction results in a new measurement date, with compensation cost equal to the intrinsic value of the new stock awards.
- The guidance above is believed to be contrary to past existing practice but is not subject to a specific prospective application date.

## Issue 5

*Choosing to obtain shareholder approval for a stock compensation award even if the company is not required to do so.*

- The measurement date for stock compensation awarded contingent upon shareholder approval cannot occur until such approval is obtained, regardless of whether the company is required to seek approval or volitionally chooses to do so.
- The guidance above is not subject to a specific prospective application date.

## Issue 6

*Dividends on restricted stock that are forfeited unless the underlying award vests.*

- Cash payments (such as dividend equivalents) that are paid currently or contingent upon vesting do not result in variable award accounting for an otherwise fixed award.

- The guidance above is not subject to a specific prospective application date.

## Issue 7

*The recognition of compensation cost for fixed awards that vest on a "pro rata," rather than "cliff," basis.*

- The accelerated recognition methodology prescribed by FASB Interpretation No. 28 is required only for variable awards.

- Compensation cost for fixed awards with pro rata vesting can be recognized either on a pro rata or accelerated basis, so long as the methodology is consistently applied.

- The guidance above is a codification of what is believed to be existing practice and is not subject to a specific prospective application date.

## Issue 8

*Whether the "accounting attributes" of stock options or awards exchanged in a pooling-of-interests transaction or a purchase business combination "carry forward" from the combining company/acquiree to the issuer/acquirer, e.g., whether variable award accounting carries forward from the combining company/acquiree to the issuer/acquirer if the combining company/acquiree previously accounted for the exchanged stock options as variable awards (e.g., because of a prior "repricing").*

- The accounting attributes of exchanged stock options or awards carry forward from the combining company to the issuer in a pool-

ing-of-interest transaction, but do *not* carry forward from the
acquiree to the acquirer in a purchase business combination (i.e.,
stock options or awards exchanged in a purchase business combination are accounted for as "new awards").

- The guidance above applies prospectively to exchanges of awards
that occur after November 16, 2000.

## Issue 9

*The subsequent repurchase of stock options or awards that were previously
exchanged in a purchase business combination, e.g., an acquirer issues stock
options in exchange for outstanding vested and nonvested stock options of an
acquiree and subsequently repurchases those options.*

- The subsequent repurchase (the six-month holding period requirement is not relevant) of stock options or awards that were *fully vested*
at the consummation date of the combination is accounted for as a
treasury stock transaction, i.e., the reacquisition of a residual equity interest; any excess of the repurchase price over the fair value
of the vested awards is accounted for as compensation cost.

- The subsequent repurchase of stock options or awards that were
*nonvested* at the consummation date is accounted for by allocating a
portion of the repurchase price to a treasury stock transaction and
a portion to compensation cost.

- The portion of the repurchase price allocated to the treasury stock
transaction is equal to the *expired* percentage of the vesting period
of the award at the consummation date of the combination; any
excess of the allocated price over the fair value of the vested portion of the award is recognized as compensation cost.

- The portion of the repurchase price allocated to compensation cost
is equal to the *remaining* vesting period of the award at the consummation date of the combination; the amount of the allocated price
that is ultimately measured and recognized as compensation cost is
determined in accordance with the guidance for award settlements
provided in FASB Interpretation No. 44. In measuring compensation cost under that guidance, the "intrinsic value of the award (if

any) at the original measurement date" is the amount allocated to unearned compensation in accounting for the combination.

- If 40% of the vesting period for a nonvested award has expired, for example, 40% of the repurchase price is allocated to the treasury stock transaction and 60% is allocated to the determination of compensation cost.

- The subsequent repurchase of vested and nonvested stock options or awards has no effect on the previous purchase accounting for the combination, i.e., the purchase price is not "remeasured."

- The guidance above applies prospectively to repurchases of stock options or awards that occur after November 16, 2000.

## Issue 10

*The subsequent modification of stock options or awards that were previously exchanged in a purchase business combination, e.g., an acquirer issues stock options in exchange for outstanding vested and nonvested stock options of an acquiree and subsequently modifies those stock options.*

- The EITF withdrew its tentative conclusion on this issue and did not reach a consensus (no further EITF discussion is planned).

- The SEC Observer stated that, in financial statements filed with the SEC, the subsequent modification of stock options or awards previously exchanged in a purchase business combination (regardless of whether vested or nonvested at the date the combination was consummated) should be accounted for as a modification under APB Opinion No. 25 and FASB Interpretation No. 44 consistent with all other modifications of employee stock compensation.

## Issue 11

*The subsequent forfeiture of nonvested stock options or awards that were previously exchanged in a purchase business combination.*

- If an award is forfeited before vesting because the employee fails to fulfill an obligation, total compensation cost for the award is reduced to zero by decreasing compensation cost in the period of forfeiture.

- The subsequent forfeiture of nonvested stock options or awards has no effect on the previous purchase accounting for the combination, i.e., the purchase price is not remeasured.
- The guidance above applies prospectively to forfeitures of awards that occur after November 16, 2000.

## Issue 12

*Whether there are circumstances in which the exchange of parent-company stock options or awards for subsidiary-company stock options or awards should be accounted for by the purchase method (as the acquisition of a minority interest) rather than a modification as prescribed in Issue 1.*

- If the exchange involves subsidiary-company stock options or awards that were outstanding when the parent company first gained control of the subsidiary (and not subsequently modified), the exchange is accounted for by the purchase method rather than as a modification (i.e., the fair value of exchanged parent-company stock options or awards is included as part of the purchase consideration for the subsidiary).
- For all other exchanges, the modification guidance in Issue 1 is applicable.
- The guidance above applies prospectively to exchanges of awards that occur after November 16, 2000.

## Issue 13

The date that should be used by an acquirer in a purchase business combination to (1) value the stock options or awards exchanged as part of the purchase consideration and (2) measure the intrinsic value (if any) of the exchanged stock options or awards for purposes of allocating a portion of the purchase price to unearned compensation cost.

- The purchase price valuation date is determined in accordance with EITF Issue No. 99-12 (generally a reasonable period of time before and after the announcement date of the combination).

- The intrinsic value is determined at the consummation date of the combination.

- The guidance above applies prospectively to exchanges of awards that occur after November 16, 2000.

## Issue 14

The exchange of acquirer stock options or awards in a purchase business combination for nonvested stock options or awards of an acquiree that are held by nonemployees of the acquiree, and the grantees became nonemployees of the acquiree in a prior spinoff transaction.

- The fair value of stock options or awards issued by the acquirer is allocated entirely to the purchase price, with no allocation of the purchase price to unearned compensation cost (or some other cost).

- However, if the fair value of the acquirer's stock options or awards exceeds the fair value of the exchanged awards in the acquiree, such excess is accounted for as a "cost" and not as part of the purchase price.

- The subsequent forfeiture of nonvested stock options or awards has no effect on the previous purchase accounting for the combination, i.e., the purchase price is not remeasured.

- The guidance above applies prospectively to exchanges of awards that occur after November 16, 2000.

## Issue 15

*An employee's agreement to reimburse an employer for the United Kingdom National Insurance Contribution (NIC) tax imposed on employers for an employee's option profit at exercise.*

- The agreement results in variable award accounting for the stock options if the reimbursement payment is not fixed and is contingent upon option exercise, regardless of whether the agreement is part of the original terms of the award or pursuant to a modification of the award.

- The agreement does not result in variable award accounting for the stock options if the reimbursement payment is for a *fixed amount* of NIC tax; the exercise price for purposes of computing the award's intrinsic value at the measurement date (the measurement date is the grant date if the agreement is part of the original terms of the award, or the modification date if the agreement is pursuant to a modification of the award and it is possible to conclude that further changes in the exercise price will not occur in the future, consistent with the guidance in Issue 26) is equal to the sum of (1) the stated exercise price of the award and (2) the fixed amount of the NIC tax reimbursement.

- The guidance above is not subject to a specific prospective application date.

## Issue 16

A *"statutory transfer"* of an employer's NIC tax liability to an employee in the original terms *of the award.*

- The statutory transfer has no accounting consequence.

- The guidance above is not subject to a specific prospective application date.

## Issue 17

A *statutory transfer of an employer's NIC tax liability to an employee through a modification to an otherwise fixed award.*

- The statutory transfer results in only in a new measurement date (as opposed to variable award accounting); the new exercise price is equal to the sum of (1) the stated exercise price of the award, and (2) the award's intrinsic value at the modification date multiplied by the employer's applicable NIC tax rate.

- Importantly, the modification is not deemed to be an "effective cancellation" of the award pursuant to the "cancellation and replacement" provisions of FASB Interpretation No. 44 (because the modification is not expected to "reduce the likelihood of exercise").

- The guidance above applies prospectively to modifications to out-standing awards that occur after November 16, 2000.

## Issue 18

*An employee or nonemployee service provider holds nonvested stock options or awards with terms that provide for the acceleration or continuation of vesting upon a change in status to or from an employee, i.e., the awards are not forfeited upon a change in status; a change in status occurs (and services continue to be provided) and the nonvested awards are otherwise modified coincident with the change.*

- Compensation cost is remeasured at the modification date using the method of accounting appropriate for the grantee's status *before* the change, and is recognized at the modification date only for the portion of newly measured compensation cost attributable to the *expired* vesting period of the award; in addition, variable award accounting is required prospectively for this portion of the award if the modification is a repricing that occurs concurrent with a change in status from employee to nonemployee.

- Compensation cost is also remeasured at the modification date using the method of accounting appropriate for the grantee's status *after* the change (as if the award is newly granted) and is recognized over the remaining vesting period only for the portion of newly measured compensation cost attributable to the *remaining* vesting period of the award.

- The guidance above applies prospectively to changes in grantee status that occur after November 16, 2000.

## Issue 19

*An employee holds nonvested stock options or awards with terms that provide for the continuation of vesting upon termination of employment; termination of employment occurs and the former employee* no longer provides services *to the company.*

- There is no accounting consequence if the former employee no longer continues to provide services to the company; if the terms of the award provide for continued vesting under the all termination scenarios, however, the award is deemed to be granted for past services and any measured compensation cost for a fixed award is recognized in full at grant.

- If the former employee continues to provide services to the company, (1) compensation cost is remeasured at the change in status date using the method of accounting appropriate for the grantee's status *after* the change (i.e., the fair value method), and is recognized over the remaining vesting period only for the portion of newly measured compensation cost attributable to the *remaining* vesting period of the award, and (2) no adjustment is made to compensation cost (if any) recognized before the change in status under the prior method of accounting, unless the grantee fails to fulfill an obligation.
- The guidance above applies prospectively to changes in grantee status that occur after November 16, 2000.

## Issue 20

*An employee who holds nonvested stock options or awards terminates employment and no longer provides services to the company; what happens upon termination of employment if either (1) the awards would have been forfeited by their terms but are modified to continue or accelerate vesting or (2) the awards would have been retained by their terms (either through an acceleration or continuation of vesting) but are otherwise modified.*

- Compensation cost is remeasured at the modification date using the method of accounting appropriate for the grantee's status *before* the change (i.e., the intrinsic value method), and is recognized in full at the change in status because no remaining services are required by the employee, i.e., the award is substantively vested.
- If the former employee continues to provide service to the company and the awards are modified to continue or accelerate vesting, (1) compensation cost is remeasured at the modification date using the method of accounting appropriate for the grantee's status *after* the change (i.e., the fair value method), and is recognized either imme-

diately (if the award becomes fully vested as a result of the modification) or over the remaining vesting period of the award, and (2) compensation cost (if any) recognized before the modification date (under the prior method of accounting) is reversed in full at the change in status (i.e., the original award is deemed to be forfeited).

- If the former employee continues to provide service to the company and the awards are modified *other than* to continue or accelerate vesting, (1) compensation cost is remeasured at the modification date using the method of accounting appropriate for the grantee's status *before* the change (i.e., the intrinsic value method) and is recognized at the modification date only for the portion of newly measured compensation cost attributable to the *expired* vesting period of the award (in addition, variable award accounting is required prospectively for this portion of the award if the modification is a repricing that occurs concurrent with a change in status from employee to nonemployee), and (2) compensation cost is also remeasured at the modification date using the method of accounting appropriate for the grantee's status *after* the change (i.e., the fair value method) and is recognized over the remaining vesting period only for the portion of newly measured compensation cost attributable to the *remaining* vesting period of the award.

- The guidance above applies prospectively to changes in grantee status that occur after November 16, 2000.

## Issue 21

*The appropriate accounting in the separate financial statements of a consolidated subsidiary for stock options or awards granted by the subsidiary to employees of another member of the consolidated group, e.g., to the parent company or another subsidiary.*

- The fair value of the stock options or awards (as measured on the *grant date*) is recognized as a *dividend* to the controlling company, with an offsetting contribution to capital.

- The guidance above applies prospectively to new awards granted after November 16, 2000.

## Issue 22

*The appropriate accounting in the separate financial statements of a consolidated subsidiary for stock options or awards granted to employees of the subsidiary by another member of the consolidated group (other than the parent company).*

- The fair value of the stock options or awards (as ultimately measured on the award's *vesting date*) is recognized as compensation cost over the service period with an offsetting contribution to capital.

- The guidance above applies prospectively to new awards granted after November 16, 2000.

## Issue 23(a)

*An employer's right to repurchase shares from an employee at fair value within six months after option exercise or share issuance when the right is not contingent upon future events, i.e., an "active" employer call right on "immature" shares.*

- FASB Interpretation No. 44 provides that variable award accounting is required for otherwise fixed stock options or awards with an employer call right, if that right is *expected to be exercised* within six months after option exercise or share issuance; if the call right is not expected to be exercised, variable award accounting is not required.

- The presence of an active employer call right does not result in variable award accounting if a "continuing assessment" can be made that the repurchase of immature shares is "not expected to occur." The assessment should be based on (1) the employer's stated representation not to call immature shares and (2) whether that representation is consistent with "all other relevant facts and circumstances," including the frequency and circumstances under which immature shares have been called in the past, the existence of legal or other limitations that may proscribe exercise of the call right, and whether the employer is a closely held or private company.

- If the above assessment cannot be made, variable award accounting is required until the earlier of (1) when the expectation of repurchase no longer exists, (2) when the call right expires or is exercised, or (3) when the shares subject to the call right are no longer immature; compensation cost recognized while the award was accounted for as a variable award should not be reversed if the award is subsequently accounted for as a fixed award.

- The guidance above applies prospectively to new awards granted (or new repurchase features added) after January 18, 2001.

## Issue 23(b)

*An employer's right to repurchase shares from an employee at fair value within six months after option exercise or share issuance when the right is contingent upon future events (such as death, disability, or retirement), i.e., a "contingent" employer call right on immature shares.*

- The presence of a contingent employer call right does not result in variable award accounting if the contingent event is "outside the control" of the employer and the event is not expected to occur; the assessment should be made on a individual grantee-by-grantee basis throughout the contingency period, taking into consideration all relevant facts and circumstances.
- The accounting guidance for active employer call rights in Issue 23(a) should be followed if the contingent event is either (1) within the control of the employer or (2) outside the control of the employer and the event is expected to occur.
- The guidance above applies prospectively to new awards granted (or new repurchase features added) after January 18, 2001.

## Issue 23(c)

*An employee's right to sell shares back to the company at fair value within six months after option exercise or share issuance when the right is contingent upon future events, i.e., a contingent employee put right on immature shares.*

- FASB Interpretation No. 44 provides that variable award accounting is required for otherwise fixed stock options or awards with an employee put right if that right *can be exercised* at the volition of the employee within six months after option exercise or share issuance.

- The presence of a contingent employee put right does not result in variable award accounting if the contingent event is outside the control of the employee and the event is not expected to occur; the assessment should be made on an individual grantee-by-grantee basis throughout the contingency period, taking into consideration all relevant facts and circumstances.

- If the contingent event is either (1) within the control of the employee or (2) outside the control of the employee and the event is expected to occur, variable award accounting is required until the earlier of (1) when the expectation of repurchase no longer exists, (2) when the put right expires or is exercised, or (3) when the shares subject to the put right are no longer immature; compensation cost recognized while the award was accounted for as a variable award should not be reversed if the award is subsequently accounted for as a fixed award.

- The guidance above applies prospectively to new awards granted (or new repurchase features added) after January 18, 2001.

## Issue 23(d)

*The accounting consequence of share repurchase features (i.e., employer call and employee put rights) with a repurchase price* at other than fair value.

- For public companies, the presence of an active or contingent employer call right at other than fair value results in variable award accounting until the earlier of the expiration or exercise of the call right (regardless of whether the call right is exercisable within six months after option exercise or shares issuance), unless the call right is not expected to be exercised; an active call right at less than fair value is always presumed to be exercised (and thus variable award accounting is required), and a contingent call right for which the contingent event is outside the control of the employer and is not expected to occur is never presumed to be exercised (and thus variable award accounting is not required); the accounting guidance for active employer call rights in Issue 23(a) should be followed for all other active and contingent employer call right scenarios.

- For public companies, the presence of an active or contingent employee put right (other than a put right at a *fixed premium* over the stock price) results in variable award accounting until the earlier of expiration or exercise of the put right (regardless of whether exercisable within six months of option exercise or share issuance), unless the put right is contingent on future events that are outside the control of the employee and are not expected to occur; a put right at a fixed premium over the stock price results in either (1) variable award accounting (until the earlier of expiration or exercise of the put right, or six months after option exercise or share issuance) if the put right is exercisable within six months after option exercise or share issuance or (2) additional compensation cost in an amount equal to the fixed premium (to be recognized over the vesting period) if the put right is *not* exercisable within six months after option exercise or share issuance.

- For nonpublic companies, the guidance above for public companies applies until the employee has made a "substantial investment" in the underlying award; if the call or put right is expected to be exercised within six months after the substantial investment is made, variable award accounting continues until the earlier of (1) expiration or exercise of the call or put right or (2) six months after the date the substantial investment is made.

- The guidance above applies prospectively to new awards granted (or new repurchase features added) after January 18, 2001.

## Issue 24

*The grant of an "in-the-money" stock option that occurs more than six months after the cancellation of an "out-of-the-money" stock option, e.g., "six months and one day."*

- Variable award accounting is required for the new in-the-money stock option (because there is a presumption that "an agreement or implied promise existed to compensate the grantee for stock price increases" after cancellation of the out-of-the-money stock option), unless relevant facts and circumstances clearly indicate the two awards are not related; factors to consider include (1) the grantor's previous stock compensation grant practices, (2) the length of time between cancellation and issuance, and (3) the treatment of the affected grantee population.

- Variable award accounting is not required if the new stock option is granted "at-the-money," even if the new exercise price equals or approximates the stock price at the date the out-of-the-money stock option was canceled.

- The guidance above applies prospectively to new awards granted after January 18, 2001.

## Issue 25

*The original terms of an otherwise fixed stock option provide for exercise with a full recourse note that may not bear a market interest rate on the date of exercise.*

- Variable award accounting is required until the stock option is exercised, is forfeited, or expires unexercised; rationale is that the exercise price is not fixed for a recourse note arrangement that does not bear market terms.

- Variable award accounting is not required if the interest rate is established *upon exercise* (rather than grant), provided the interest rate is "a market rate based on the rate environment at the date of exercise (based on the credit standing of the grantee)."

- The guidance above applies prospectively to new awards granted (or outstanding awards modified) after January 18, 2001.

## Issue 26

*The accounting consequence of modifying an otherwise fixed stock option to* increase *the exercise price or* reduce *the number of shares.*

- Such a modification results in either a new measurement date or variable award accounting, depending on all relevant facts and circumstances.

- A new measurement date is required if it is possible to conclude that further changes to the exercise price or number of shares will not occur in the future, such as when unusual modifications are sometimes made to comply with the regulatory environment (e.g., refer to Issue 17).

- Variable award accounting is required if there is no practical way to ascertain whether further changes to the exercise price or number of shares will occur in the future; factors to consider include (1) whether the award has been similarly modified in the past, (2) whether the modification is related to the grantee's job performance, or (3) whether other factors indicate that similar modifications are possible in the future.

- The guidance above applies prospectively to modifications to outstanding awards that occur after January 18, 2001.

## Issue 27

*Whether a cash bonus and stock option award should be accounted for as a "combined award" if the cash bonus is contingent on a factor that may be a "proxy" for exercise.*

- Consistent with FASB Interpretation No. 44, variable award accounting is not required if the cash bonus is not contingent on option exercise.

- Variable award accounting is required, however, if the cash bonus is contingent upon the employee's *sale* of stock received from a previous option exercise (the exercise of the stock option is one of two conditions that must be met in order for the employee to receive the cash bonus).

- The guidance above is not subject to a specific prospective application date.

## Issue 28(a)

*The appropriate accounting in the separate financial statements of a consolidated subsidiary for stock compensation granted to its employees based on tracking stock that is referenced to either that subsidiary or another subsidiary of the consolidated group.*

- Tracking stock is considered for legal and accounting purposes to be equity of the parent company, and not equity of the unit or subsidiary to which the stock tracks.

- If the tracking stock is "substantive," the stock compensation should be accounted for in the separate financial statements of a subsidiary under APB Opinion No. 25 (and not FASB Statement No. 123); a tracking stock is considered substantive if it is publicly traded (other criteria may also lead to the determination that the tracking stock is substantive).

- If the tracking stock is not substantive, the award should be accounted for as a cash-based or formula arrangement in both the separate subsidiary and consolidated financial statements.

- The guidance above applies prospectively to new awards granted (or outstanding awards modified) after January 18, 2001.

## Issue 28(b)

*The exchange of outstanding stock options based on the tracking stock in one member of a consolidated group for stock options in another member of the same group when the exchange does not occur in connection with a nonreciprocal equity restructuring.*

- The guidance for stock option exchanges in Issue 1 should be followed if the tracking stock is considered substantive (as defined in Issue 28(a)).

- The guidance above applies prospectively to new awards granted (or outstanding awards modified) after January 18, 2001.

## Issue 29(a)

*How to account for income tax benefits from the exercise of nonqualified stock options that were previously issued in a nontaxable purchase business combination and that were* fully vested *at the date the combination was consummated.*

- The income tax benefit (i.e., the option gain at exercise multiplied by the company's tax rate) is recognized as a *reduction* to the purchase price of the acquired business to the extent that the deduction reported for tax purposes does not exceed the fair value of the awards included in the purchase price; the tax benefit of any remaining excess tax deduction is treated as a contribution to capital.

- The guidance above applies prospectively to exchanges of awards that occur after January 18, 2001.

## Issue 29(b)

*How to account for income tax benefits from the exercise of nonqualified stock options that were previously issued in a purchase business combination and that were* nonvested *at the date the combination was consummated.*

- The accounting guidance for recognizing income tax benefits in Issue 29(a) should be followed for the portion of the nonvested stock options attributable to the *expired* vesting period of the awards at the consummation date.

- The accounting guidance for recognizing income tax benefits for stock options granted *absent a business combination* (i.e., the "normal" income tax accounting rules) should be followed for the portion of the nonvested stock options attributable to the *remaining* vesting period of the awards at the consummation date.

- The guidance above applies prospectively to exchanges of awards that occur after January 18, 2001.

## Issue 30

*Modifying an otherwise fixed stock option to add a "short-term inducement" to exercise the stock option, e.g., a cash bonus or increased number of shares that expires after two weeks.*

- Variable award accounting is required until the modified award is exercised, is forfeited, or expires unexercised (because the exercise price and/or number of shares are no longer fixed).
- The guidance above is not subject to a specific prospective application date.

## Issue 31

*Whether fixed award accounting applies to a stock option with an exercise price that is denominated in a currency other than the "functional" currency of the grantor.*

- Variable award accounting is required if the exercise price is denominated in multiple currencies or in a currency other than the currency of the "primary economic environment of either the employer or the employee" (because the exercise price is not fixed).
- The guidance above applies prospectively to new awards granted after January 18, 2001.

## Issue 32

*How to account for employer payroll taxes associated with the exercise of stock options that were previously exchanged in a purchase business combination and that were vested at the date the combination was consummated.*

- A liability (and corresponding cost) for employer payroll taxes incurred on employee stock compensation should be recognized on the date of the event triggering the income recognition and payment of tax to the taxing authority (e.g., on the date of exercise for a nonqualified stock option), consistent with the guidance in EITF Issue No. 00-16.

- The subsequent recognition of the liability and cost has no effect on the previous purchase accounting for the combination, i.e., the purchase price is not remeasured.

- The guidance above applies prospectively to exchanges of stock options or awards in purchase business combinations that are consummated after April 19, 2001.

## Issue 33(a)

*How to account for the "early exercise" of a stock option if the employer has a contingent repurchase or "call" right until the award is vested with a strike price equal to the lesser of fair value of the stock at the call date or the original exercise price paid by the employee (sometimes referred to as a "California Style" stock option).*

- The contingent call right is in substance a forfeiture provision that preserves the original vesting schedule of the award and results in no adverse accounting consequences for the early exercise an otherwise fixed stock option, provided the call right (1) expires at the end of the original vesting period of the award, (2) becomes exercisable only if a termination event occurs that would have caused the award to be forfeited, and (3) is priced at the *lower of* the employee's exercise price or the fair value of the stock on the date the call is exercised; an acceleration of vesting occurs if the employee terminates employment before vesting and the employer fails to exercise the call right.

- In addition, the shares received upon early exercise are not considered "issued" for purposes of computing basic earnings per share (EPS) or determining whether the shares are "mature."

- The guidance above applies regardless of whether the early exercise provision is pursuant to the original terms of the stock option or added through a subsequent modification of the award.

- The guidance above applies prospectively to stock options granted or modified after July 19, 2001.

## Issue 33(b)

*Same fact pattern as Issue 33(a) except that the strike price for the employer call right is based solely on the original exercise price paid by the employee (i.e., not the lesser of fair value of the stock at the call date or the original exercise price).*

- The early exercise is *not* recognized for accounting purposes if the employer strike price is based solely on the original exercise price of the stock option; rather, any cash paid for the exercise price is considered a deposit or prepayment of the exercise price that should be recognized by the employer as a liability.
- The stock options should only be accounted for as exercised when the awards become vested and the employer repurchase right lapses; an acceleration of vesting occurs if the employee terminates employment before vesting and the employer fails to exercise the call right.
- The guidance above applies prospectively to stock options granted or modified after March 21, 2002.

## Issue 34

*Whether there are circumstances under which the exercise of a stock option with a full recourse note should not be accounted for as an exercise of the option award.*

- The legal form of a recourse loan should be respected (and thus the option exercise should be recognized), unless (1) the employer has legal recourse to the employee's other assets but does not intend to seek repayment beyond the shares issued, (2) the employer has a history of not demanding repayment of loan amounts in excess of the fair value of the shares, (3) the employee does not have sufficient assets or other means (beyond the shares) to justify the recourse nature of the loan, or (4) the employer has accepted a recourse note upon option exercise and subsequently converted the recourse note to a nonrecourse note; in addition, all other relevant facts and circumstances should be evaluated when determining whether the note should be accounted for as nonrecourse, including whether the loan is ultimately forgiven or whether a portion of the exercise price can be paid with a nonrecourse loan and the remainder with a recourse loan.

- If the facts and circumstances indicate the loan arrangement is non-recourse in substance, the arrangement continues to be accounted for as a stock option in accordance with the guidance in EITF Issue No. 95-16 (that is, the exercise is not recognized for accounting purposes).

- The guidance above applies prospectively to fixed stock options that are exercised after July 19, 2001.

## Issue 35

*How to account for a stock option that is exercised with a recourse note* negotiated at the date of exercise, *if the terms of the note or another agreement provide that the note will be forgiven in whole or in part if specified "substantive" performance goals are achieved, i.e., a loan forgiveness arrangement.*

- Provided the performance goals are substantive and the stock option is considered exercised in accordance with Issue 34, variable award accounting is required for one day (the date of exercise) by analogy to the guidance in Issue 25; rationale is that the exercise price is not fixed for a recourse note arrangement that does not bear market terms.

- Further, any amount of the loan actually forgiven is recognized as additional compensation cost.

- The EITF did not address the accounting consequence of a recourse note forgiveness arrangement that is based on specified performance goals that are *not* substantive, but presumably the option exercise would *not* be recognized (and thus variable award accounting would continue beyond exercise) pursuant to the guidance in Issue 34.

- The EITF also did not address the accounting consequence of a re-course note forgiveness arrangement that *is embedded in the terms of an option agreement* (either through the original terms of the award or a subsequent modification) rather than issued in conjunction with option exercise, but presumably the same variable award accounting would apply (commencing on the date the arrangement is entered into) because the exercise price is not fixed.

- The EITF also did not address the accounting consequence of a recourse note forgiveness arrangement that is based on [presumably substantive] *continued service* rather than "specified substantive performance goals," but presumably the same variable award accounting would apply because the exercise price is not fixed.

- The above guidance applies prospectively to exercises of stock options with recourse notes that occur after November 15, 2001.

## Issue 36(a)

*The accounting consequence of an employer "offer" to cancel existing fixed stock options and, upon acceptance of the offer, grant replacement stock options with a lower exercise price* within six months *of the cancellation date of the existing options, i.e., an offer to "reprice" existing stock options.*

- The employer *offer* results in variable award accounting for *all* existing stock options subject to the offer.

- Variable award accounting commences when the offer is made, and for stock options that are retained because the offer is declined, continues until the options are exercised, are forfeited, or expire unexercised.

- The same accounting treatment applies to existing stock options even if the replacement awards are in the form of restricted stock; refer to Issue 39(a).

- The guidance above applies prospectively to employer offers that occur after July 19, 2001.

## Issue 36(b)

*How to apply the "cancellation and replacement" guidance in FASB Interpretation No. 44 when an employer offer to reprice* is accepted *by the employee.*

- Variable award accounting commences at the offer date for all existing stock options subject to the employer offer, consistent with the guidance in Issue 36(a).

- Further, because the existing stock options are subject to variable award accounting due to the deemed repricing in Issue 36(a), upon acceptance of the offer and cancellation of the existing stock options, *any* new stock options granted during the six-month look-back look-forward period are eligible to be replacement awards subject to variable award accounting treatment (not just new stock options with a *lower* exercise price).

- The guidance above applies prospectively to employer offers that occur after July 19, 2001.

## Issue 36(c)

*The accounting consequence of an employer offer to cancel existing fixed stock options, and upon acceptance of the offer, grant new replacement stock options with an "at-the-money" exercise price more than six months after the cancellation date of the existing stock options.*

- The offer results in no adverse accounting consequences for existing stock options subject to the offer, provided the six-month "safe harbor" provisions of FASB Interpretation No. 44 are satisfied (in substance, the employer has only offered to "cancel" the existing stock options, not "reprice" the options).

- But refer to Issue 39(b) if the replacement awards are in the form of restricted stock; the offer is deemed to be a repricing requiring variable award accounting in accordance with Issue 36(a).

- The guidance above applies prospectively to employer offers that occur after July 19, 2001.

## Issue 36(d)

*Whether the length of the offer period (e.g., a one-year offer period) or the existence of multiple cancellation offers would affect the conclusion reached in Issue 36(c).*

- A lengthy offer period or the existence of multiple offers does not adversely affect the conclusion reached in Issue 36(c) other than to extend the "window of evaluation" as defined in Issue 36(e) below for identifying replacement awards.

- The guidance above applies prospectively to cancellation offers that occur after November 15, 2001.

## Issue 36(e)

*The appropriate date that stock options are deemed to be canceled when an employer makes an offer to cancel existing stock options and replace with new awards, e.g., the offer date, the acceptance date, or the date the stock options are legally canceled and all regulatory requirements for cancellation are met.*

- Stock options are deemed canceled on the date that all legal and regulatory requirements for cancellation are met, such as the date an election to cancel can no longer be revoked.

- Further, the window of evaluation for purposes of identifying replacement awards begins six months before commencement of the offer period (that is, the date the offer is communicated to employees), continues *through* the offer period, and ends six months after the stock options are legally canceled.

- The guidance above applies prospectively to award cancellations that occur after November 15, 2001.

## Issue 37(a)

*How to account for the intrinsic value at the original measurement date of a nonvested fixed stock option that is canceled and not replaced with a new award.*

- Consistent with the compensation cost recognition guidance for fixed awards in FASB Interpretation No. 44, companies should (1) *always* recognize as compensation cost the intrinsic value of the award (if any) at the original measurement date and (2) *never* reverse previously measured compensation cost for a fixed award unless the employee "fails to fulfill an obligation."

- The guidance above applies prospectively to fixed stock options that are canceled after July 19, 2001.

## Issue 37(b)

*How to account for the settlement of nonvested stock awards with new "at-the-money" stock options.*

- The transaction is deemed to be an "upward repricing," and the guidance in Issue 26 should be followed to determine whether a new measurement date or variable award accounting is required for the new stock options.
- Regardless of how the new stock options are accounted for, the original intrinsic value of the settled nonvested awards should be recognized as compensation cost consistent with the guidance in Issue 37(a) (that is, the previously measured cost should *not* be reversed),
- The guidance above applies prospectively to nonvested stock awards that are settled after July 19, 2001.

## Issue 38

*Clarification of the term "substantial investment" as it relates to a nonpublic company's share repurchase feature based on other than fair value.*

- Share repurchase features based on other than fair value for nonpublic companies may not meet the substantial investment criterion (even if the employee invests an amount at least equal to the formula share repurchase price calculated at the date of grant) if the formula results in a *de minimis* employee investment that does not approximate fair value (because the employee does not share in the *risks* of ownership).
- Share repurchase features that result in an employee investment of zero *never* meet the substantial investment criterion.
- The guidance above applies prospectively to employee investments that occur after November 15, 2001.

## Issue 39(a)

*The accounting consequence of an employer offer to cancel existing fixed stock options and, upon acceptance of the offer, grant restricted stock within six months of the cancellation date of the existing stock options (same fact pattern as Issue 36(a) except the replacement awards are in the form of restricted stock rather than stock options).*

• The employer offer results in variable award accounting for all existing stock options subject to the offer, consistent with the guidance in Issue 36(a).

• Variable award accounting commences when the offer is made, and for stock options that are retained because the offer is declined, continues until the options are exercised, are forfeited, or expire unexercised.

• The guidance above applies prospectively to employer offers that occur after November 15, 2001.

## Issue 39(b)

*The accounting consequence of an employer offer to cancel existing fixed stock options, and upon acceptance of the offer, grant restricted stock more than six months after the cancellation date of the existing stock options (same fact pattern as Issue 36(c) except the replacement awards are in the form of restricted stock rather than stock options).*

• The six-month safe harbor is not relevant if replacement awards are in the form of restricted stock because the grantees are protected from future stock price increases regardless of when the restricted stock is granted (that is, an offer to grant restricted stock after six months is in substance the same as an offer to grant restricted stock immediately upon cancellation of the stock options).

• Thus, consistent with the repricing guidance in Issue 36(a), the employer offer results in variable award accounting for all existing stock options subject to the offer; variable award accounting commences when the offer is made, and for stock options that are retained because the offer is declined continues until the options are exercised, are forfeited, or expire unexercised.

- The guidance above applies prospectively to employer offers that occur after November 15, 2001.

## Issue 39(c)

*The accounting consequence of an employer offer to cancel and regrant stock options (consistent with the fact pattern in Issue 36(c)) if the offer provides for reinstatement of the canceled options (or acceleration of the grant of new replacement awards) during the six-month safe harbor period upon the occurrence of certain events, such as death, involuntary termination, or change-in-control.*

- Consistent with the guidance in Issue 36(e), the cancellation date and related commencement of the six-month look-forward period cannot occur until the canceled stock options can no longer be reinstated or the grant of new replacement awards can no longer be accelerated, which is generally the same date the new replacement awards are granted (resulting in variable award accounting if the new replacement awards are stock options).
- The guidance above applies prospectively to employer offers that occur after November 15, 2001.

## Issue 39(d)

*The accounting consequence of an employer offer to cancel and regrant stock options (consistent with the fact pattern in Issue 36(c)) if the number of new replacement stock options differs from the number of canceled stock options, i.e., a six-month safe harbor cancellation and replacement at other than a 1:1 replacement ratio.*

- Variable award accounting is *not* required provided the number of new at-the-money replacement stock options is not determined by a formula that is either directly or indirectly linked to changes in the market price of the underlying stock.

- Variable award accounting *is* required for the new replacement stock options (regardless of when granted) if judgement indicates that the formula is intended to compensate the grantee for stock price increases during the six-month safe harbor period.

- The guidance above applies prospectively to employer offers that occur after January 24, 2002.

## Issue 39(e)

*The accounting consequence of an employer offer to cancel and regrant stock options if a portion of the new replacement stock options are granted immediately upon cancellation (to protect the grantee against stock price increases during the six-month safe harbor period) and a portion are granted more than six months after cancellation (to avoid variable award accounting for that portion of the grant).*

- Variable award accounting is required for the initial replacement stock options granted immediately upon cancellation because the six-month safe harbor period is violated.

- Variable award accounting also is required for a portion of the remaining replacement stock options granted more than six months after cancellation if the exercise period for the initial replacement stock options expires *within* six months of the grant of the remaining replacement stock options, consistent with the indirect repricing guidance in FASB Staff Announcement Topic No. D-91; the number of remaining replacement stock options subject to variable award accounting is equal to the number of initial stock options granted (fixed award accounting applies to any remaining replacement stock options in excess of the number of initial replacement stock options granted).

- Variable award accounting is *not* required for any of the remaining replacement stock options granted more than six months after cancellation if either (1) the exercise period for the initial replacement stock options expires *more than six months after* the grant of the remaining replacement stock options or (2) the initial stock options are granted in the form of restricted stock, regardless of when granted (because restricted stock is always viewed as a "replacement award," rather than as "consideration for stock price increases" during the six-month safe harbor).

- The guidance above applies prospectively to replacement awards granted after November 15, 2001.

## Issue 39(f)

*The accounting consequence of canceling existing stock options without providing substantial consideration in exchange for the cancellation.*

- FASB Interpretation No. 44 provides that an "effective cancellation" is deemed to occur if, at the time a replacement award is granted, an agreement exists (in any form) to cancel or settle an existing stock option at a specified future date.

- The cancellation of stock options in exchange for consideration that is not substantial suggests that there was an implied agreement to provide value through other means; thus, a rebuttable presumption exists that the cancellation is linked to a previous stock option with a lower exercise price, which if not overcome, would required variable award accounting for the previous grant (even if granted more than six months before the cancellation).

- The guidance above applies prospectively to award cancellations that occur after November 15, 2001.

## Issue 39(g)

*The accounting consequence of "truncating" the exercise period of stock options.*

- FASB Interpretation No. 44 provides that an effective cancellation is deemed to occur if existing stock options are modified to "reduce or eliminate the likelihood of exercise," such as by reducing (or truncating) the exercise period of the options.

- Whether an exercise period truncation actually reduces or eliminates the likelihood of exercise, however, depends on whether the stock options are in-the-money or underwater.

- The truncation of in-the-money stock options generally should *not* reduce the likelihood of exercise (in fact, the truncation may actually *increase* the likelihood of exercise), and thus should not result in an effective cancellation of the options; judgment should be applied in evaluating relevant facts and circumstances when making this determination.

- The truncation of underwater stock options does reduce the likelihood of exercise, however, resulting in an effective cancellation and a window of evaluation for identifying replacement awards that begins six months before announcement of the truncation (or six months before the event triggering the truncation if the truncation is pursuant to the embedded terms of the option) and ending six months after the options expire.

- Further, variable award accounting is required for stock options that could expire *before vesting* because of a truncation provision for reasons other than the grantee's termination of employment (because the number of shares is not fixed); variable award accounting applies until the stock options become vested (refer to Issue 45 which clarifies the guidance in FASB Staff Announcement Topic No. D-91).

- The guidance above applies prospectively to stock options granted or truncated after November 15, 2001.

## Issue 40(a)

*Whether a grantee who provides services to an LLC (or other pass-through entity) should be considered an employee for purposes of accounting for capital- or equity-based compensation (profits interest awards) granted by the LLC.*

- The grantee of a profits interest award should be considered an employee if the grantee qualifies as a common law employee; the fact that the LLC does not classify the grantee as an employee for payroll tax purposes is not relevant.

- The guidance above applies prospectively to profits interest arrangements of an LLC (or other pass-through entity) after November 15, 2001.

## Issue 40(b)

*If a grantee of a profits interest award is considered to be an employee for purposes of applying APB Opinion No. 25, whether that award should be accounted for as a fixed or variable award.*

- A profits interest award should be accounted for based on its substance, taking into consideration all relevant facts and circumstances including the investment required, liquidation or prepayment provisions, and provisions for the realization of value.

- The guidance above applies prospectively to profits interest awards granted after March 21, 2002.

## Issue 41

*The exchange of outstanding stock options based on a company's tracking stock (or any class of stock) into stock options in the company's surviving common stock when the exchange does* not *occur in connection with a nonreciprocal equity restructuring.*

- The guidance for stock option exchanges in Issues 1 and 28(b) should be followed in event of the elimination or exchange of *any* class of stock (other than a nonreciprocal transfer), including a change from a multiple-class to a single-class capital structure, an exchange of nonvoting for voting common stock, and the elimination of one of several tracking stocks.

- The guidance above applies prospectively to award modifications that result from the elimination of (1) tracking stock that occur after November 15, 2001, and (2) any other class of stock that occur after January 24, 2002.

## Issue 42(a)

*Whether noncompensatory stock compensation plans in tax jurisdictions outside the United States (such as Save-As-You-Earn or "SAYE" plans in the United Kingdom) are noncompensatory under APB Opinion No. 25 if the purchase discount is more than 15%.*

- Compensatory plan accounting is required under APB Opinion No. 25 if the purchase discount exceeds 15% of the stock price *at grant.*

- The guidance above applies prospectively to new grants that occur after January 24, 2002.

## Issue 42(b)

*Whether noncompensatory stock compensation plans in tax jurisdictions outside the United States (such as SAYE plans in the United Kingdom) are noncompensatory under APB Opinion No. 25 if the exercise period is greater than 27 months.*

- Compensatory plan accounting is required under APB Opinion No. 25 if the exercise period exceeds (1) 27 months in the case of an exercise price based on the stock price *at grant* or (2) 5 years in the case of an exercise price based on the stock price *at exercise.*

- The guidance above applies prospectively to new grants that occur after January 24, 2002.

## Issue 42(c)

*Whether noncompensatory stock compensation plans in tax jurisdictions outside the United States (such as or SAYE plans in the United Kingdom) are "fixed" under APB Opinion No. 25 if the grantee can elect to cancel (and forfeit) one contract and enter into a new contract if offered by the employer.*

- The employer offer to enter into a new contract within six months at a lower exercise price results in variable award accounting for all existing awards subject to the offer, consistent with the guidance in Issue 36(a).

- Variable award accounting commences when the offer is made, and for awards that are retained because the offer is declined, continues until the awards are exercised, are forfeited, or expire unexercised; variable award accounting is also required for any new awards granted to the extent that previous higher priced awards are canceled.

- The guidance above applies prospectively to employer offers that occur after January 24, 2002.

## Issue 43

*The accounting consequence of an company's failure to adjust outstanding stock options or awards in connection with a nonreciprocal equity restructuring.*

- FASB Interpretation No. 44 provides that there is no accounting consequence for otherwise fixed stock options or awards that are modified (regardless of whether the modification is pursuant to the original terms of the award or not) to adjust the exercise price and/or number of shares coincident with an "equity restructuring" (defined as a nonreciprocal transaction such as a stock dividend, spinoff, stock split, rights offering, or large nonrecurring dividend that causes a company's stock price to decrease), provided (1) the aggregate intrinsic value of the award is not increased and (2) the ratio of exercise price to the market price per share is not *reduced.*

- If the embedded terms of stock options or awards *require* equitable adjustments in connection with an equity restructuring but the company nevertheless *fails to do so,* the accounting consequence of such failure is a deemed modification resulting in either (1) a repricing requiring variable award accounting if the effect is a *reduction* in exercise price or (2) either a new measurement date or variable award accounting (depending on all relevant facts and circumstances consistent with the guidance in Issue 26) if the effect is an *increase* in exercise price; further, if the failure to adjust awards results in a reduced likelihood of exercise, the awards are deemed to be effectively canceled similar to the guidance in Issue 39(g).

- If in connection with a stock split, reverse stock split, or stock dividend treated as a stock split, the embedded terms of [presumably underwater] stock options provide for equitable adjustment to the exercise price but *not* the number of shares, any such adjustment is deemed to be a repricing requiring variable award accounting (because the aggregate *negative* intrinsic value is reduced).

- If the embedded terms of stock options or awards are *silent* in regard to equitable adjustments in connection with an equity restructuring (or if adjustments are at the *discretion* of the company), the accounting guidance above applies in event of a stock split, reverse stock split, or stock dividend treated as a stock split; the accounting guidance above also applies in event of a spinoff or large nonrecurring cash dividend unless relevant facts and circumstances provide sufficient evidence of a reason *not* to make equitable adjustments, such as the existence of legal or contractual prohibitions (e.g., debt convenants).

- The guidance above applies prospectively to equity restructurings that occur after November 15, 2001.

## Issue 44

*The accounting consequence of an acquiring company's decision* not *to assume outstanding target company stock options or awards in connection with a purchase business combination.*

- So long as no legal obligation exists to assume outstanding target company stock options or awards, those awards and any new awards granted by the acquiring company should not be linked for accounting purposes (and any target awards not assumed would not be deemed to be "effectively canceled" for purposes of the cancellation and replacement guidance in FASB Interpretation No. 44).

- However, post-acquisition awards should be accounted for as consideration for the purchase business combination if there is evidence of an oral or implied agreement at acquisition to grant new awards to target grantees in exchange for target company stock options or awards after the acquisition (a grant made within one year of acquisition to target employees that differs significantly from the acquiring company's normal grant pattern may provide evidence of such an implied agreement).

- The guidance above applies prospectively to business combinations consummated after March 21, 2002.

## Issue 45

*Whether a measurement date occurs at grant date if stock options could expire before vesting.*

- The guidance in FASB Staff Announcement Topic No. D-91 is clarified to provide that variable award accounting is required for stock options that could expire *before vesting* because of a truncation provision for reasons other than the grantee's termination of employment (because the number of shares is not fixed); variable award accounting applies until the stock options become vested (also refer to the guidance in Issue 39(g)).

- The guidance above applies prospectively stock options that could expire before vesting after November 15, 2001.

## Issue 46

*The accounting consequence of a transferability provision on an otherwise fixed stock option or award (either pursuant to the original terms of the award or through a subsequent modification of the award).*

- A transferability provision (either pursuant to the original terms of the award or through a subsequent modification of the award) does not result in an accounting consequence, unless all relevant facts and circumstances indicate that either (1) the subsequent transfer results in a reacquisition of the award by the employer (for example, the transfer results in the payment of cash or other consideration by the employer to reacquire the award) or (2) the employer facilitates the transfer to circumvent existing accounting rules, as would be the case if the employer uses the employee as a conduit to transfer the award to a nonemployee service provider of the employer (thereby avoiding the accounting requirements of FASB Statement No. 123 and EITF Issue No. 96-18).

- The guidance above applies prospectively to awards granted or modified after March 21, 2002.

## Issue 47

*The original terms of an otherwise fixed stock option provide a reload feature for shares used to satisfy minimum statutory tax withholding obligations upon exercise, i.e., a "tax reload" feature.*

- The scope of EITF Issue No. 90-7 is amended to provide that tax reloads (consistent with the fact pattern in this Issue 47) do *not* result in variable award accounting.
- Further, the shares tendered to satisfy minimum statutory tax withholding obligations need not satisfy the six-month holding period requirement in EITF Issue No. 84-18.
- The guidance above applies prospectively to new awards granted after January 24, 2002.

## Issue 48

*The accounting consequence of a "cashless exercise" of a stock option effected through a broker.*

- There is no accounting consequence for a cashless exercise of a stock option effected through a broker that is *unrelated* to the grantor, provided that the employee makes a valid exercise of the stock option and the grantor concludes the employee is the legal owner of all option shares (that is, the employee assumes market risk from the moment of exercise until the broker effects the sale on the open market); if the employee is never the legal owner of the shares, the stock option would be in substance a stock appreciation right (SAR) for which variable accounting would be required (such as when it is illegal for individuals in certain countries to own shares in foreign corporations or for companies in certain countries to allow share ownership by foreign nationals).

- If the broker is a *related party* of the grantor, there is no accounting consequence for a cashless exercise provided (1) the employee takes legal ownership of the option shares as discussed above, (2) the broker-dealer assisting the exercise is a substantive entity with operations that are separate and distinct from those of the grantor (except in circumstances in which the broker-dealer itself is the grantor) and sells the option shares on the open market, and (3) the cashless exercise process is the same whether or not the exercise is being performed for a related entity or an independent entity.

- The guidance above applies as of June 30, 2002, to all outstanding awards and prospectively to all new awards that permit broker-assisted exercise.

## Issue 49

*Adjusting outstanding stock options or awards in connection with a nonreciprocal equity restructuring when the outstanding awards have nega-tive intrinsic value.*

- There is no adverse accounting consequence if the two requirements of Issue 1 are satisfied, that is, (1) the aggregate negative intrinsic value is not *reduced*, and (2) the ratio of exercise price to market price per share is not *reduced*.

- If the second requirement of Issue 1 is satisfied but the aggregate negative intrinsic value is reduced (that is, the first requirement is not satisfied), the exchange is accounted for as the grant of a new award (the number of additional stock options that would have been issued to maintain the same aggregate negative intrinsic value) and a deemed cancellation of those additional awards that would be subject to the look-back look-forward cancellation and replacement guidance in FASB Interpretation No. 44 and Issue 39(f).

- If the second requirement of Issue 1 is *not* satisfied, variable award accounting is required for the entire exchanged award.

- The guidance above applies prospectively to equity restructurings that occur after January 24, 2002.

## Issue 50

*The accounting consequence of converting a recourse note (that represents consideration for a previous stock compensation transaction) to a note considered to be nonrecourse.*

- The conversion should be accounted for as the repurchase of the shares previously exercised with a recourse note, and the simultaneous grant of a new stock option in return for a nonrecourse note.

- The repurchase amount is equal to the sum of (1) the then-current principal balance of the recourse note, (2) accrued interest (if any), and (3) the intrinsic value of the new stock option.

- If the repurchase amount exceeds the fair value of the option shares repurchased and the note conversion occurs *more than* six months after option exercise or share issuance, the repurchase is accounted for as a treasury stock transaction, and compensation cost is recognized for the excess of the repurchase amount over the fair value of the shares on the conversion date.

- If the repurchase amount exceeds the fair value of the option shares repurchased and the note conversion occurs *within* six months after option exercise or share issuance, the repurchase is accounted for as the acquisition of immature shares, and compensation cost is recognized in accordance with the guidance for award settlements provided in FASB Interpretation No. 44. In measuring compensation cost under that guidance, the "amount of cash paid to the employee" is the repurchase amount as defined above

- If the fair value of the option shares repurchased exceeds the repurchase amount (and the employee is not required to pay the difference), the grantor is deemed to have forgiven that portion of the recourse note, and thus all existing and future recourse notes issued in conjunction with option exercises should be accounted for as nonrecourse notes pursuant to the guidance provided in Issue 34.

- The new stock option is accounted for under the nonrecourse note guidance provided in EITF Issue No. 95-16.

- The guidance above applies prospectively to recourse/nonrecourse note conversions that occur after March 21, 2002.

## Issue 51

*How to account for a stock option that is based on the stock of an unrelated entity.*

- The EITF reached a consensus that this issue is not within the scope of APB Opinion No. 25 or FASB Statement No. 123 because the underlying stock is not an equity instrument of the employer/ grantor.

- The EITF in Issue No. 02-08 decided that the fair value of such an option award should be accounted for as a "derivative" under FASB Statement No. 133 in the determination of net income (both during and subsequent to vesting).

Chapter 5

# FASB Statement No. 123

In 1993, the FASB proposed that the fair value of stock-based awards be included in a company's income statement. That raised a considerable outcry from companies relying heavily on options as a compensation strategy, because of the negative impact on their income statements. After much debate and controversy, the FASB agreed to recommend that companies recognize the fair value of stock-based employee compensation as compensation expense in their income statements, but not require that they do so. Instead, the costs could simply be disclosed in a footnote. This chapter addresses how companies should deal with accounting for stock-based employee compensation under these rules.

In October 1995, the FASB issued Statement No. 123, "Accounting for Stock-Based Compensation," bringing closure to the FASB's 11-year project on stock compensation accounting. Statement 123 *requires* all companies to change what they disclose about their employee stock-based compensation plans, *recommends* that they change how they account for these plans (by recognizing their fair value in the financial statements), and *requires* those companies who do not change their accounting to disclose (in a footnote to the financial statement) what their earnings and earnings per share would have been if their accounting had changed.

Historically, companies have reported stock-based compensation under Opinion 25, which requires companies to measure compensation cost using the "intrinsic value method." In the case of a typical nonqualified stock option, the compensation cost is measured at the time that both the exercise price and the number of shares are fixed and determinable. Thus, in a typical stock option grant, assuming that at the date of grant the exercise price equals the fair market value, this results in no compensation charge to the income statement (as explained in chapter 2).

Statement 123 was developed in response to criticism of the existing rules under Opinion 25 for producing anomalous results and for measuring the cost of stock options using only the intrinsic value component of fair value. Statement 123 is based on the precept that a stock option grant has an inherent value, i.e., its "fair value." Thus, the notion is that a stock option grant with an initial intrinsic value of zero (fair market value of underlying stock on the date of grant – exercise price = $0) has a fair value because of its potential, at some point over the life of the option, to be "in the money" and result in value to the option holder.

By only recommending, not requiring, that companies change how they account for their employee stock-based compensation plans, the FASB has preserved the existing accounting rules. Companies who do not follow the FASB's recommendation will thus continue to follow Opinion 25. Therefore, for fiscal years beginning after December 15, 1995, companies that elect to continue accounting for stock option grants and other equity awards under Opinion 25 are required to disclose pro forma net income and earnings per share as if they had implemented Statement 123. Additionally, all companies, whether they follow Opinion 25 or Statement 123 accounting, must provide the extensive disclosures about stock-based compensation required by Statement 123.

As anticipated, very few companies initially elected to adopt the recognition requirements of Statement 123 for stock-based employee compensation. Most companies chose instead to continue to report their results using Opinion 25 and, therefore, must provide the additional footnote disclosures required by Statement 123. Recently, however, there has been mounting pressure on companies to adopt the provisions of Statement 123. As a result of corporate scandal and shareholder activism demanding better reporting and more transparent financial statements, there has been a flurry of activity as almost 200 companies have publicly announced their intentions to adopt Statement 123 for the accounting for stock-based employee compensation. There will be continued pressure on companies to voluntarily adopt the provisions of Statement 123. Additionally, it is believed by many that the FASB will impose Statement 123 (or similar) accounting on companies in the very near future. However, at this time, it appears that the majority of companies are taking a wait-and-see approach and will continue to report under Opinion 25.

## Overview of Statement 123

This chapter describes the fair value method of accounting for stock-based employee compensation under Statement 123. Statement 123 permits a company to choose either a fair value-based method or the Opinion 25 intrinsic value-based methodology of accounting for its stock-based employee compensation arrangements. Statement 123 requires pro forma disclosures of net income and earnings per share computed as if the fair value-based method had been applied in financial statements of companies that continue to account for such arrangements under Opinion 25.

Statement 123 applies to all stock-based employee compensation plans in which an employer grants shares of its stock or other equity instruments to employees, except for employee stock ownership plans (ESOPs). The statement also applies to plans in which the employer incurs liabilities to employees in amounts based on the price of the employer's stock (e.g., stock appreciation rights). Statement 123 also applies to transactions in which a company issues stock options or other equity instruments for services provided by nonemployees, such as consultants and bankers, or to acquire goods or services from outside suppliers or vendors. Companies were required to adopt Statement 123 for nonemployee transactions entered into after December 15, 1995.

One objective of the FASB's stock compensation accounting project was to level the playing field between fixed awards and performance awards. The irony is that Opinion 25 encourages companies to grant fixed awards, which do not incorporate a performance measure, as this generally results in no charge to earnings. By contrast, performance-based awards, which, in theory, should be viewed more favorably by shareholders, usually result in variable accounting under Opinion 25 and a charge to earnings if the price of the stock increases.

The discussion of the fair value-based accounting methodology throughout this chapter applies equally to measuring compensation cost for those companies that adopt the fair value method for accounting purposes, and to measuring compensation cost for companies that continue to report under Opinion 25 and are required to disclose pro forma net income and earnings per share as if the recognition requirements of Statement 123 had been used to account for stock-based employee compensation.

## Major Provisions

The most significant provision of Statement 123 is the FASB's decision to permit companies to disclose the fair value of equity awards through a footnote disclosure rather than to recognize the value in the financial statement; if it were recognized in the financial statement, most companies' reported net income would be adversely affected. The footnote disclosure requirements of the statement, which recently were amended by FASB Statement No. 148, *Accounting for Stock-Based Compensation—Transition and Disclosure,* apply to all companies regardless of the method used to account for stock compensation arrangements and can become very cumbersome. An example of the disclosure footnote is provided below under the heading "Example of a Footnote Disclosure." Other significant provisions of Statement 123 include the following:

- Compensation cost is recognized (in pro forma net income for companies electing to accounting for stock-based employee compensation under Opinion 25) for most stock-based employee compensation arrangements.

- Stock options and other equity instruments issued to nonemployees and other suppliers of goods or services should be accounted for based on fair value. As stated earlier, companies are required to apply Statement 123 for stock options and other equity instruments issued to nonemployees regardless of whether a company adopts Statement 123 or continues to report under Opinion 25 for its employee stock-based accounting. Further guidance regarding the accounting for stock-based compensation to nonemployees is included in EITF Issue No. 96-18, "Accounting for Equity Instruments That Are Issued to Other Than Employees for Acquiring, or in Conjunction with Selling, Goods or Services."

- Compensation cost for all stock-based compensation awards granted to employees is measured on the date of grant except in instances where it is not possible to estimate fair value at grant date, such as when the exercise price of a stock is indexed to the underlying stock price, or when the award is a liability (e.g., the employee could require the employer to cash settle the award).

- Compensation cost is measured based on the estimated fair value of the equity instruments granted. The estimated fair value of stock options is measured using a pricing model that considers specified factors. Under Opinion 25, compensation cost is determined by the intrinsic value at the measurement date.

- Fluctuations in the underlying stock price after the date of grant do not change compensation cost determined at grant date.

- Most existing broad-based employee stock purchase plans (such as Internal Revenue Code Section 423 plans) will be compensatory. Only certain plans with a small purchase discount, generally 5% or less, and no option-like features will be treated as noncompensatory.

## Example of a Footnote Disclosure

Exhibit 5-1 (see following pages) is a financial statement footnote prepared pursuant to Statement 123. The hypothetical company is a public company that has elected to continue to account for its employee stock-based compensation plans under Opinion 25. If the company had accounted for all stock-based employee compensation under Statement 123, the pro forma disclosures would not be required.

# Exhibit 5-1: Sample Footnote Disclosure

## Footnote 1. Summary of Significant Accounting Policies

The Company has elected to account for stock options and other equity awards issued to employees under APB Opinion No. 25. [The pro forma disclosures should be here and presented in the manner required by Statement 148]

## Footnote 10. Stock-Based Compensation Plans

The Company has two stock option plans, the 1993 Top Executive Plan (the "1993 Plan") and the 1996 Middle Manager Plan (the "1996 Plan"), plus an employee stock purchase plan (the "1994 Plan"). The Company accounts for these plans under APB Opinion No. 25, under which no compensation cost has been recognized. The following table illustrates the effect on net income and earnings per share if the company had applied the fair value recognition provisions of FASB Statement No. 123, *Accounting for Stock-Based Compensation,* to stock-based employee compensation.

| | Year Ended December 31 | | |
| --- | --- | --- | --- |
| | 2003 | 2002 | 2001 |
| Net income, as reported | $ 479,300 | $ 407,300 | $ 347,790 |
| Deduct: Total stock-based employee compensation expense determined under fair value method for all awards, net of related tax effects | (18,902) | (12,747) | (10,962) |
| Pro forma net income | $ 460,398 | $ 394,553 | $ 336,828 |
| Earnings per share: | | | |
| Basic—as reported | $2.66 | $2.29 | $1.97 |
| Basic—pro forma | $2.56 | $2.22 | $1.91 |
| Diluted—as reported | $2.02 | $1.73 | $1.49 |
| Diluted—pro forma | $1.94 | $1.68 | $1.44 |

Additionally, the 2003 pro forma amounts include $1,268,500 related to the purchase discount offered under the 1994 Plan, which was subsequently amended. The pro forma cost of the amended plan is zero.

The Company may sell up to 10,000,000 shares of stock to its full-time employees under the 1994 Plan. The Company has sold or will sell 522,000 shares, 710,000 shares, and 811,000 shares in 1996, 1997, and 1998, respectively, and will sell 2,626,000 shares through December 31, 2003. The Company sells shares at 95% (85% in 2003) of the stock's market price at date of purchase. The weighted average fair value of shares sold in 2003 was $27.

The Company may grant options for up to 2,000,000 shares under the 1993 Plan and 5,000,000 shares under the 1996 Plan. The Company has granted options on 1,660,000 shares and 3,775,000 shares, respectively, through December 31, 2003. Under both Plans the option exercise price equals the stock's market price on date of grant. The 1993 and 1996 Plan options vest after three and four years, respectively, and all expire after eight years.

A summary of the status of the Company's two stock option plans on December 31, 2001, 2002, and 2003, and changes during the years then ended is presented in the table and narrative below:

|  | 2001 | | 2002 | | 2003 | |
|---|---|---|---|---|---|---|
|  | Shares (000's) | Wtd. Avg. Ex. Price | Shares (000's) | Wtd. Avg. Ex. Price | Shares (000's) | Wtd. Avg. Ex. Price |
| Outstanding at beginning of year | 2,505 | $20 | 2,575 | $22 | 2,613 | $25 |
| Grant | 700 | 27 | 720 | 30 | 700 | 33 |
| Exercised | (470) | 17 | (432) | 19 | (453) | 20 |
| Forfeited | (160) | 22 | (235) | 26 | (450) | 26 |
| Expired | – | | (15) | 31 | (50) | 32 |
| Outstanding at end of year | 2,575 | 22 | 2,613 | 25 | 2,360 | 27 |
| Exercisable at end of year | 930 | 18 | 1,088 | 19 | 1,060 | 21 |
| Weighted average fair value of options granted | $8.25 | | $8.81 | | $9.95 | |

# Exhibit 5-1: Sample Footnote Disclosure (cont'd)

925,000 of the 2,360,000 options outstanding at December 31, 2003, have exercise prices between $17 and $25, with a weighted average exercise price of $20 and a weighted average remaining contractual life of 3.3 years. All of these options are exercisable. The remaining 1,435,000 options have exercise prices between $25 and $33, with a weighted average exercise price of $31 and a weighted average remaining contractual life of 6 years. 135,000 of these options are exercisable; their weighted average exercise price is $27.

The fair value of each option grant is estimated on the date of grant using the Black-Scholes option pricing model with the following weighted-average assumptions used for grants in 2001, 2002, and 2003, respectively: risk-free interest rates of 6.0%, 6.7%, and 6.4% for the 1993 Plan options and 6.3%, 7.0%, and 6.9% for the 1996 Plan options; expected dividend yields of 3.5%, 3.5%, and 3.65%; expected lives of 5.4, 4.9, and 6.1 years for the 1993 Plan options and 5.7, 5.0, and 5.2 years for the 1996 Plan options; and expected stock price volatility of 30%, 33%, and 34%.

With respect to the company's transactions with employees, the sample footnote was prepared under the assumption that there were no options granted with exercise prices either above or below the market price of the company's stock, no performance-based plans, and no modifications of previously granted awards. All of these situations require additional disclosures.

## Implications

The changes required by Statement 123 could affect employers' financial statements in many ways. Companies that historically have granted fixed stock options to employees or have established broad-based plans, such as Section 423 stock purchase plans, generally will recognize a charge to earnings (either in the financial statements or in the pro forma net income disclosures). The effect on net income (or pro forma net income), whether positive or negative, will be magnified for companies that incorporate stock-based compensation awards as a key component in their compensation programs. Table 5-1 summarizes the differences between Opinion 25 and Statement 123.

## Measurement of Awards

Statement 123 requires compensation cost for all stock-based compensation awards, including most plans currently considered noncompensatory under Opinion 25 (i.e., broad-based plans), to be measured based on fair value.

Under Opinion 25, compensation cost for fixed and variable stock-based awards is measured by the excess, if any, of the fair market value of the stock underlying the award over the amount the individual is required to pay. This is the intrinsic value concept. Compensation for fixed awards is measured at the grant date, when both the number of shares and the price the holder is required to pay is fixed and definite. The compensation cost for variable awards is estimated until both the number of shares an individual is entitled to receive and the exercise or purchase price are known (the measurement date).

**Table 5-1. Comparison Between Accounting Under Opinion 25 and Statement 123**

| COMPENSATION VEHICLE | OPINION 25 | STATEMENT 123 |
|---|---|---|
| **Fixed Stock Options** | | |
| *Measurement Date* | Grant date | Same |
| *Compensation Amount* | Excess of quoted or fair market value over exercise price | Estimated fair value at grant date using an accepted option pricing model |
| **Performance-Based Stock Plans** | | |
| *Measurement Date* | Date both the number of shares and share price are known (generally the end of the performance period) | Grant date (unless fair value cannot be reasonably measured) |
| *Compensation Amount* | Intrinsic value at measurement date | Estimated fair value at grant date using an accepted option pricing model |
| *Effect of Changes in Stock Price after Grant Date* | Final compensation cost based on the ending quoted or fair market value of the stock at the end of the performance period | No effect—the expense is "locked in" at the date of grant |
| **Restricted Stock Plans (No Performance-Based Conditions)** | | |
| *Measurement Date* | Grant date | Same |
| *Compensation Amount* | Quoted or fair market value of nonvested shares less amount employee is required to pay | Same |

*(continued on next page)*

| COMPENSATION VEHICLE | OPINION 25 | STATEMENT 123 |
|---|---|---|
| **Employee Stock Purchase Plans**<br><br>*Compensation Cost* | Noncompensatory if plan is broad-based, discount is 15% or less, and if an option, term is limited to a reasonable period (generally 27 months) | Noncompensatory if plan is broad-based, discount is 5% or less, and plan has no option features<br><br>Cost equals fair value of option component |
| **Cash-Only Plans (e.g., SARs and Phantom Plans)**<br><br>*Measurement Date* | Settlement date | Same |
| *Compensation Amount* | Cash paid to employee at settlement date | Same |
| **Cash Settlements of Stock-Based Awards**<br><br>*Employer May Issue Stock or Cash at Its Discretion* | Payment of cash upon settlement considered final measure of compensation | Cash paid to repurchase award (not in excess of fair value) generally is charged to equity, however, a pattern of cash settlements may suggest that the substantive terms of the plan require cash settlement |
| *Employer Is Obligated to Pay Cash at Employee's Election* | Accounted for as a liability with compensation cost determined at date of settlement | Same |
| **Earnings per Share: Calculation of Weighted Average Shares Outstanding**<br><br>*Basic Earnings per Share* | Include only vested common shares | Same |
| *Diluted earnings per share* | Include all dilutive common stock equivalents outstanding | Same |

## Fair Value of the Consideration Exchanged

The goal in measuring stock-based employee compensation is to estimate the fair value of the consideration exchanged at the time the transaction occurs.

Current accounting principles require that a stock-based transaction
be accounted for based on the fair value of the consideration received
or the fair value of the equity instruments issued, whichever is more
reliably measurable. For transactions with employees, Statement 123
presumes that the fair value of employee services is not readily determinable and thus requires measurement of the fair value of the equity
instruments issued.

The method of determining the fair value of an equity instrument
varies by instrument. Fair values of shares of stock come from quoted
stock prices or, in the absence of a trading market, appraisals. Fair values of stock options or their equivalents must be estimated using op-
tion-pricing models (e.g., Black-Scholes or binomial models) that incorporate the following six assumptions:

1.  The fair market value of the underlying stock on the date of grant.

2.  The exercise price of the option.

3.  The risk-free interest rate (the rate on a zero-coupon Treasury secu-
    rity with a term equal to the expected life of the option).

4.  The expected life of the option. The FASB recognized that most op-
    tions are exercised before the expiration of the contractual option
    term (typically 10 years). Therefore, the FASB permits companies to
    use a shorter term that will more accurately reflect the expected life
    of the option until exercise. Typically, the estimate is based on the
    company's exercise history.

5.  The expected volatility of the underlying stock (an estimate of the
    future stock price variability of the stock over a period equal in length
    to the expected life of the option). Private companies are permitted
    to use a "minimum value method" to value stock options, which
    excludes the impact of volatility from the calculated value.

6.  The expected dividend yield. This should reflect the company's ex-
    pectation of future dividend yield as a percentage of stock price over
    a period of time equal to the expected life of the option.

The first three assumptions are relatively easy to determine, but the estimation of the last three assumptions can be a significant challenge. In estimating the expected volatility of and dividends on the underlying stock, the objective is to approximate the expectations of market participants. Similarly, the objective in estimating the expected lives of employee stock options is to approximate the expectations that an outside party with access to detailed information about employees' exercise behavior likely would develop based on information available at the grant date. Both the volatility and the dividend yield components should reflect reasonable expectations commensurate with the expected life of the option. While the determination of these assumptions is highly subjective, the estimated should be supported by objective historical or market information.

The option pricing models should not consider restrictions on transferability or the risk of forfeiture. Restrictions on transferability are addressed through the use of an expected life of the option (the reason employees exercise options early and forfeit remaining time value is because they cannot transfer the options). The risk of forfeiture is reflected in the recognition methodology.

The option pricing models are used only to value stock options. Restricted stock awards will be measured using the fair market value of the stock (assuming the stock is publicly traded), or the estimated market price if it is not traded publicly.

## Option Pricing Models

The most commonly used methodologies for valuing publicly traded options include the Black-Scholes model and the Cox-Ross-Rubinstein binomial pricing models. Private companies can use the Minimum Value Method, which does not incorporate a stock volatility element. Basically, the Minimum Value Method is a present value methodology that calculates the value of the option as the sum of the intrinsic value and the present value of the ability to defer the exercise price of the option over its term.

The Black-Scholes and binomial pricing models are based on complex mathematical formulas. The Black-Scholes model was originally developed for relatively short-lived publicly traded options on stocks that do not pay dividends. The binomial model was developed to encompass a broader variety of conditions.

## Effect of the Six Variables on the Option Pricing Values

The impact of each assumption on the stock option value (assuming all other variables remain fixed) is as follows:

- *Exercise price of the stock option:* An increase in the exercise price results in a decrease in the value of the stock option.
- *Fair market value of the company stock:* An increase in the fair market value of the stock results in an increased stock option value.
- *Risk-free rate:* An increase in the risk-free rate results in an increase in the stock option value.
- *Expected dividend yield:* An increase in the dividend yield results in a lower stock option value.
- *Expected stock option term:* An increase in the term results in an increase in the stock option value.
- *Expected stock volatility:* An increase in the volatility results in an increase in the stock option value. This variable typically has the greatest impact on changes in the stock option value.

### Expected Volatility

Volatility is the measure of the amount that a stock's price (including dividends) has fluctuated (historical volatility) or is expected to fluctuate (expected volatility) during a specified period. Volatility is expressed as a percentage; a stock with an annualized volatility of 25% would be expected to have its year-end stock price fall within a range of plus or minus 25 percentage points of its beginning of the year stock price two-thirds of the time. Because of their greater risk, stocks with high volatility provide option holders with greater economic upside potential and result in higher option values under the Black-Scholes and binomial option pricing models.

Statement 123 suggests that historical volatility be calculated over the most recent period equal to the expected life of the options. Thus, if the weighted-average expected life of the options is seven years, historical volatility should be calculated for the seven years immediately preceding the option grant. However, under Statement 123, companies are not expected to calculate stock volatility without considering the extent that historical experience reasonably predicts future experience.

To that extent, companies are permitted to adjust historical volatility if, as a result of changes specific to the company, historical volatility is not representative of expected volatility. For example, historical volatility may be adjusted in the following circumstances:

- A company that significantly changes its line of business (e.g., as the result of merger and acquisition activity).

- A company that has been a takeover target and as a result has seen dramatic spikes in the stock price. To the extent this is not "normal" or expected behavior for the future, a company should make an adjustment for this period of stock history.

## Expected Dividends

The assumption about expected dividends should be based on publicly available information. While standard option pricing models generally call for expected dividend yield, most models may be modified to use an expected dividend amount rather than a yield. If a company uses expected payments, any history of regular increases in dividends should be considered.

## Expected Option Lives

The expected life of an employee stock option award should be estimated based on reasonable facts and assumptions on the grant date. The following factors should be considered:

- The average length of time similar grants have remained outstanding.
- The vesting period of the grant.
- The expected volatility of the underlying stock.

The expected life can be no less that the vesting period and, in most circumstances, will be less than the contractual life of the option. Additionally, experience indicates that employees tend to exercise options on highly volatile stocks earlier than options on stocks with low volatility.

While use of a longer expected life results in a greater estimated value of a stock option, the relationship between value and expected life is not linear. For example, a two-year option is worth less than twice as much as a one-year option if all other assumptions are equal. Generally, the majority of an option value is recognized in the first seven years of the option term. As a result, calculating estimated option values based on a single weighted-average life that includes widely differing individual lives may misstate the value of the entire award. Therefore, companies are encouraged to group optionees into relatively homogeneous groups and calculate the related option values based on appropriate weighted-average expectations for each group. For example, if executives at the senior management level tend to hold their options longer than middle management, and nonmanagement employees tend to exercise their options sooner than other plan participants, Statement 123 indicates that it would be appropriate to segment the employees into different bands for purposes of calculating the weighted-average estimated life of the options. An example is provided later in this chapter.

It should be noted that stock option awards issued to nonemployees must consider EITF Issue No. 96-18, *Accounting for Equity Instruments That Are Issued to Other Than Employees for Acquiring, or in Conjunction with Selling Goods or Services*. For nonemployee stock options, the contractual life of the option must be used to estimate fair value of the award. The measurement date is the earlier of (1) the performance commitment date or (2) the date the services have been completed. If the penalty for not meeting the performance commitment is the forfeiture of the award, the performance commitment will not be satisfied. In many cases, the measurement date will not occur until the options vest. Accordingly, the company will be required to remeasure the fair value of the equity award each reporting period until the completion of vesting. Assuming the stock appreciates during the service period, the compensation expense could be greater than originally anticipated. The rules under Issue 96-18 are complex and should be reviewed with the company's accountant before entering into an equity-based arrangement with a nonemployee.

## Minimum Value Method

Statement 123 indicates that a private company may estimate the value of its options without consideration of the expected volatility of its stock. This method of estimating an option's value is referred to as the Minimum Value Method, which is a present value concept. Following is an example of a Minimum Value calculation for a private company, assuming a 10-year expected life, a $50 exercise price, a 2% expected dividend yield, and a 7% risk-free rate:

| | |
|---|---|
| Current Stock Price | $ 50.00 |
| Present Value of Exercise Price | (24.83) |
| Present Value of Expected Dividends During Option Term | (7.15) |
| Estimated Option Value | $ 18.02 |

In this example, the present value of the exercise price, $50, discounted at 7% over the life of the option, would yield a value of $24.83. In theory, if an individual invested $24.83 risk-free (i.e., at 7%) for 10 years, the investor would have the amount required to exercise the option at the end of the term ($50). An investor who owned the stock, however, would have received dividends during the term of the option— a present value of $7.15. Therefore, the net benefit of deferring payment of the $50 exercise for 10 years is $18.02. If no dividends were payable, the dividend component would be removed from the equation.

## Recognition of Compensation Cost

Awards for past services (generally, awards not subject to vesting) would be recognized as a cost in the period the award is granted. Compensation expense related to awards for future services is recognized by a charge to compensation cost and a corresponding credit to equity (paid-in capital) as the services are received. The service period generally would be considered equivalent to the vesting period. Vesting occurs when the employee's right to receive the award is not contingent upon the performance of additional services or the achievement of a specified target.

*Single Option Life Approach vs. Multiple Option Life Approach*

There are different approaches to estimating and recognizing the compensation cost, depending on the structure of the option-vesting schedule. In the case of cliff vesting (a single vesting date on which all awards fully vest), compensation for these awards generally is recorded on a straight-line basis from grant date to vesting date.

Alternatively, companies also use graded vesting schedules (e.g., options vest at a rate of one-third per year over a three-year period), which allows employees to partially vest in the award over time, as if the award is really a series of individual awards, each with its own vesting period. Statement 123 permits companies to select an accounting policy to value awards subject to graded vesting as either one award with a single expected life or multiple awards with different expected lives based on the different (i.e., graded) vesting periods:

- If the award is considered to be one award (e.g., exercise habits do not vary by employee type, stock price performance, etc.) and not a series of separate grants, the service period begins at the grant date and generally ends on the last vesting date. In this circumstance, the company may choose to recognize compensation expense on a straight-line over the vesting period or based on FIN 28's accelerated approach. The company must apply this accounting policy consistently to all awards subject to graded vesting.

- A series of individual awards (as FIN 28 requires for variable plans under Opinion 25). As Statement 123 states, if there are different exercise patterns or habits among various groups of employees, using a single expected option life may result in an inaccurate estimate of total compensation expense. If viewed as separate awards, expense for each tranche is recognized separately based on the service period for each tranche (typically equal to the vesting period for that specific tranche). For example, assuming an option grant vests in equal annual tranches over a three-year period:

  - the first 33% of the grant fully vests in year 1,
  - the second 33% vests in years 1 and 2, and
  - the final tranche vests equally over years 1, 2, and 3.

The result, as illustrated further below, is that viewing the award as separate awards will result in expensing the cost faster.

The decision to select the most appropriate of the methods above is a policy decision and should consistently be applied.

Tables 5-2, 5-3, 5-4, and 5-5 illustrate the issue by comparing the Single Life Option Approach versus the Multiple Life Option Approach.

### Compensation Cost and Measurement Period

The Single Life Approach results in $35,000,000 of compensation expense over the three-year vesting cycle, compared to $34,000,000 under the Multiple Life Approach. The company must have support for using the multiple life approach, which generally is evidenced by employee exercise history.

## Adjustment of Initial Estimates

Measurement of the value of stock options at grant date generally requires estimates relative to the outcome of service- and performance-related conditions. Statement 123 adopts a grant date measurement approach for stock-based awards with service requirements or performance conditions and specifies that the estimated option value and resulting compensation cost should be adjusted for subsequent changes in the expected or actual outcome of these factors.

A performance requirement adds another condition that must be met for employees to vest in certain awards, in addition to rendering services over a period of years. Compensation cost for these awards should be recognized each period based on the best estimate whether the performance-related conditions will be met. When the award contains performance conditions that adjust the number of equity instruments to be issued under the award, the entity will make its best estimate of the number of equity instruments that will be issued. If this estimate changes, then the cumulative effect of the adjustment is recorded in the period the change occurs at the original grant date fair value of the award.

If the performance condition is the achievement of a targeted stock price or specified amount of intrinsic value, compensation expense

**Table 5-2**

| Single Life Approach | Multiple Life Option Approach |
|---|---|
| Options on 1,000,000 shares are granted to employees | 200,000 options are expected to be exercised in 3.0 years |
| Exercise price is $100 | 300,000 options are expected to be exercised in 4.0 years |
| Expected option life for all employees is 5.5 years | 500,000 options are expected to be exercised in 7.0 years |
| Fair value using a Black-Scholes model is $35 per share | Exercise price for all option is $100 |
| | Fair value calculations:* |
| |     3.0 year options - $25 |
| |     4.0 year options - $30 |
| |     7.0 year options - $40 |

\* For illustration, assumes interest rate and dividend yields are constant. In actual calculations, the variables are likely to be different. All options vest ratably over three years.

## Table 5-3. Single Life Approach—Straight Line Recognition

Options on 1,000,000 shares are granted to employees

Fair value using a Black-Scholes model is $35 per share

Total compensation cost to be expensed = $35,000,000

| Vesting Period | Number of Options | Value | Expense Period 1 | Expense Period 2 | Expense Period 3 |
|---|---|---|---|---|---|
| Year 1 | 333,333 | $35.00 | $11,666,655 | $0 | $0 |
| Year 2 | 333,333 | $35.00 | $0 | $11,666,655 | $0 |
| Year 3 | 333,334 | $35.00 | $0 | $0 | $11,666,690 |
| Annual Expense | | | $11,666,655 | $11,666,655 | $11,666,690 |
| Cumulative Expense | | | | $23,333,310 | $35,000,000 |

The illustration assumes that all shares vest—no forfeitures or terminations.

## Table 5-4. Single Life Approach—Accelerated Recognition

Options on 1,000,000 shares are granted to employees

Fair value using a Black-Scholes model is $35 per share

Total compensation cost to be expensed = $35,000,000

| Vesting Period | Number of Options | Value | Expense Period 1 | 2 | 3 |
|---|---|---|---|---|---|
| Year 1 | 333,333 | $35.00 | $11,666,655 | $0 | $0 |
| Year 2 | 333,333 | $35.00 | $5,833,328 | $5,833,328 | $0 |
| Year 3 | 333,334 | $35.00 | $3,888,897 | $3,888,897 | $3,888,897 |
| Annual Expense | | | $21,388,879 | $9,722,224 | $3,888,897 |
| Cumulative Expense | | | | $31,111,103 | $35,000,000 |

The illustration assumes that all shares vest—no forfeitures or terminations.

**Table 5-5. Multiple Option Life Approach—Accelerated Recognition**

Options on 1,000,000 shares are granted to employees

Expected option lives have been stratified by employee and expected exercise timeframe

| Vesting Period | Number of Options | Expected Life | Fair Value | Expense Period 1 | Expense Period 2 | Expense Period 3 |
|---|---|---|---|---|---|---|
| Year 1 | 200,000 | 3.0 years | $25.00 | $5,000,000 | $0 | $0 |
| Year 2 | 300,000 | 4.0 years | $30.00 | $4,500,000 | $4,500,000 | $0 |
| Year 3 | 500,000 | 7.0 years | $40.00 | $6,666,667 | $6,666,667 | $6,666,667 |
| Annual Expense | | | | $16,166,667 | $11,166,667 | $6,666,667 |
| Cumulative Expense | | | | | $27,333,333 | $34,000,000 |

The illustration assumes that all shares vest—no forfeitures or terminations.

would not be adjusted subsequently for failure to meet the condition. For awards that incorporate such features, compensation cost is recognized for employees who remain in service over the service period, regardless of whether the target stock price or amount of intrinsic value is reached. Statement 123 does indicate, however, that a target stock price condition generally affects the value of such options. Previously recognized compensation cost should not be reversed if a vested employee stock option expires unexercised.

### Modifications to Grants

Statement 123 requires that a modification to the terms of an award that increases the award's fair value at the modification date be treated, in substance, as a new award. Additional compensation cost resulting from a modification of a vested award should be recognized immediately for the difference between the fair value of the new award at the modification date and the fair value of the original award immediately before its terms are modified, based on the shorter of its remaining expected life or the expected life of the modified option. For modifications of nonvested options, compensation cost related to the original award not yet recognized must be added to the incremental compensation cost of the new award and recognized over the remainder of the employee's service period.

Exchanges of options or changes in their terms in conjunction with business combinations, spinoffs, or other equity restructurings are considered modifications under Statement 123. With regard to spinoffs and other equity restructurings, this represents a change in practice, as such modifications do not typically result in a new measurement date under Opinion 25, and therefore additional compensation expense is not recorded.

## Specific Types of Plans

### Restricted Stock

Restricted stock awards will be measured using the fair market value of the stock (assuming the stock is publicly traded), or the estimated market price if it is not traded publicly. The fair value of the restricted shares (number of shares times the fair market value of the stock) will be expensed over the vesting cycle. The accounting treatment for restricted shares follows the same principles that apply to stock options and that were explained earlier in this chapter.

## Tandem Plans and Combination Plans

Employers may have plans that offer employees a choice of receiving either cash or shares of stock in settlement of their stock-based compensation awards. Such plans are considered tandem plans. For example, an employee may be given an award consisting of a stock option and a stock appreciation right under which the employee may demand settlement in either cash or in shares of stock, and the election of one option cancels the other. Because the employee has the option to receive cash, this plan would be accounted for as a liability plan whereby total compensation cost is recognized over the service period. The amount of the liability will be adjusted each period to reflect the current stock price. If employees subsequently choose to receive shares of stock rather than receive cash, the liability is settled by issuing stock.

## Awards Requiring Settlement in Cash

Typically, an employer settles stock options by issuing stock rather than paying cash. However, under certain stock-based plans, an employer may be required to settle the awards in cash. For example, a cash stock appreciation right derives its value from the appreciation in employer stock but is ultimately settled in cash. Such plans include phantom stock plans, cash stock appreciation rights, and cash performance unit awards.

Under Opinion 25, cash paid to settle a stock-based award is the final measure of compensation cost. The repurchase of stock shortly after exercise of an option is also considered cash paid to settle an earlier award and ultimately determines compensation cost. Statement 123 indicates that awards calling for settlement in stock are considered equity instruments when issued, and their subsequent repurchase for cash would not require an adjustment to compensation cost if the amount paid does not exceed the fair value of the instrument repurchased. Awards calling for settlement in cash (or other assets of the employer) are considered liabilities when issued, and the liability and compensation cost are adjusted to equal the cash to be paid upon settlement (estimated based on the current stock price) every period until final settlement.

## Employee Stock Purchase Plans

Some companies offer employees the opportunity to purchase company stock, typically at a discount from market price. If certain conditions are met, the plan may qualify under Section 423 of the Internal Revenue Code, which allows employees to defer taxation on the difference between the market price and the discounted purchase price. Opinion 25 treats employee stock purchase plans that qualify under Section 423 as noncompensatory.

Under Statement 123, broad-based employee stock purchase plans are compensatory unless the discount from market price is relatively small and the plan has no option features. Plans that provide a discount of no more than 5% would be considered noncompensatory; discounts over this amount would be considered compensatory under Statement 123 unless the company could justify a higher discount as (1) a reasonable discount in a recurring offer of stock to stockholders, or (2) a reasonable estimate of the per-share amount of stock issuance costs avoided by not having to raise a significant amount of capital in a public offering. If a company cannot provide adequate support for a discount in excess of 5%, then the entire amount of the discount should be treated as compensation cost.

For example, if an employee stock purchase plan provides that employees can purchase the employer's common stock at a price equal to 85% of its market price as of the date of purchase, compensation cost would be based on the entire discount of 15% unless the 15% can be justified under one of the two approaches described in the preceding paragraph. In the U.S., it is unlikely that either approach would support a 15% discount.

An offer to an employee to sell stock at a discount from market price is not considered stock-based compensation if an employee stock purchase plan meets all of the following criteria:

- The discount from the market price does not exceed the greater of (1) the per-share public offering costs avoided or (2) the per-share discount that would be reasonable in a recurring stock offering, with discounts of 5% or less automatically deemed to meet these criteria. By contrast, transactions with discounts of up to 15% automatically fit within this safe harbor under Opinion 25. Discounts this large are unlikely to qualify under Statement 123.

- The company offers the arrangement to substantially all full-time employees who meet certain employment qualifications, and the terms of the participation are equitable. This condition is essentially unchanged from Opinion 25.

- The plan incorporates no option features other than the following:

  (1) Employees are permitted a short period of time—not exceeding 31 days—after the purchase price has been fixed to enroll in the plan.

  (2) The purchase price is based solely on the stock's market price at date of purchase, and employees are permitted to cancel participation before the purchase date and obtain a refund of amounts previously paid (such as those paid by payroll withholdings).

Most existing employee stock purchase plans have one or both of the following option features: (1) a plan that establishes a purchase price for the stock, gives employees a period of time to accumulate funds from payroll withholdings, and then permits employees to proceed with the purchase or receive the cash withheld, or (2) a plan that gives employees the lower of two purchase prices—for example, 85% of the lesser of the market price at the enrollment date or the market price at the purchase date. Because of these option features, as well as the fact that such plans normally offer a discount in excess of 5%, essentially all employee stock purchase plans in the U.S. are considered compensatory under Statement 123.

## Disclosures

Statement 123 supersedes the disclosure requirements under Opinion 25 and requires disclosure of the following information by employers with one or more stock-based compensation plans, regardless of whether a company has elected the recognition provisions or retained accounting under Opinion 25:

- A description of the method used to account for all stock-based employee compensation arrangements in the company's summary of significant accounting policies.

- For an entity that adopts the fair value recognition provisions of Statement 123, a description of the method of reporting the change in accounting principle if the financial statements include the period of adoption.

- A description of the plans, including the general terms of awards under the plans—such as vesting requirements, the maximum term of options granted, and the number of shares authorized for grants of options or other equity instruments.

- For each year for which an income statement is presented:

  - The number and weighted-average exercise prices of options for each of the following groups of options: those outstanding at the beginning and end of the year; those exercisable at the end of the year; and those options granted, exercised, forfeited, or expired during the year.

  - The weighted-average grant date fair value of options granted during the year. If the exercise prices of some options differ from the market price of the stock on the grant date, weighted-average exercise prices and fair values of options would be disclosed separately for options whose exercise price equals, exceeds, or is less than the market price of the stock on the date of grant.

  - The number and weighted-average grant-date fair value of equity instruments other than options (e.g., shares of nonvested stock) granted during the year.

  - A description of the method and significant assumptions used to estimate the fair values of options, including the weighted-average risk-free interest rate, expected life, expected volatility, and expected dividends.

- Total compensation cost recognized in income for stock-based compensation awards.
- The terms of significant modifications to outstanding awards.

In addition to the disclosures described above, companies that continue to apply the provisions of Opinion 25 during any period for which an income statement is presented in the financial statements should disclose the following in a tabular presentation for each year an income statement is presented (FASB Statement No. 148, *Accounting for Stock-Based Compensation—Transition and Disclosure*, requires that these disclosures be included in the financial statement footnote that includes the summary of significant accounting policies and must be presented in both annual and interim financial statements):

- Net income and basic and diluted earnings per share as reported.
- Stock-based employee compensation cost, net of the related tax effects, included in the determination of net income as reported.
- Stock-based employee compensation cost, net of related tax effects, that would have been included in the determination of net income if the fair value method had been applied to all awards.
- Pro forma net income and pro forma basic and diluted earnings per share and as if the fair value method had been applied to all awards.

For the latest balance sheet date presented:

- The range of exercise prices, as well as the weighted average exercise price.
- The weighted average contractual life.
- When the range of exercise prices is wide (the highest exceeds the lowest by 150%), segregate the ranges in meaningful categories and disclose for each range:
  - The number, weighted-average exercise price, and weighted-average remaining contractual life of the options outstanding.
  - The number and weighted-average exercise price of options currently exercisable.

Prospective method

Modified Prospective

Retroactive Restatement

*Chapter* **6**

# FASB Statement No. 123 Transition Rules

In an effort to facilitate the expected transition to Statement 123 accounting, in December 2002 the FASB issued Statement of Financial Accounting Standards No. 148, *Accounting for Stock-Based Compensation—Transition and Disclosure, an amendment of FASB Statement No. 123,* which outlines the alternative transition methods and disclosure provisions under Statement 123.

To briefly summarize Statement 148, the FASB decided to allow three alternative transition approaches for companies that adopt Statement 123 expensing in 2002 or 2003, but to eliminate one of these approaches (the Prospective Method) for companies that adopt Statement 123 for the accounting for stock-based employee compensation for fiscal years beginning after December 15, 2003.

Companies that first adopt Statement 123 for the accounting for stock-based employee compensation in fiscal years that begin on or before December 15, 2003, can select from among three alternative transition approaches: the Prospective Method, the Modified Prospective Method, or the Retroactive Restatement Approach.

*Prospective Method*   The method originally provided for in Statement 123, which applies only to awards granted or modified after the date of adoption (and not for any earlier grants, including unvested awards). This approach results in a gradual "ramp up" of compensation expense while the full effects of Statement 123 are being phased in. Many companies and financial statement users objected to this approach because reported compensation expense would not be comparable from period to period until Statement 123 was fully phased in, and urged the FASB to provide alternative transition approaches.

*Modified Prospective Method*   This is a "fresh start" approach, because the company would adopt Statement 123 for stock-based employee awards in the year the method is adopted, rather than phasing in the effects as under the Prospective Method. Under this method, previously issued financial statements would not be affected, but new statements would reflect a full transition to Statement 123 (for all grants subject to vesting, regardless of when made).

*Retroactive Restatement Approach*   Under this method, companies would restate all periods presented to recognize stock-based employee compensation cost under Statement 123 for all employee awards that are granted, modified, or settled in fiscal years beginning after December 14, 1994, and fully apply Statement 123 expense recognition concepts in the year of adoption and after. Companies are not required to restate periods that are not presented.

Companies first adopting Statement 123 for stock-based employee awards in fiscal years starting after December 15, 2003 (i.e., 2004 for calendar year companies) will only be allowed to use the second and third transition methods and will not be allowed to use the Prospective Method.

In addition, Statement 148 expands disclosure requirements for all companies reporting under Opinion 25 or Statement 123. Under the new standard, companies must report pro forma information more prominently and in a user-friendlier format in the footnotes to the financial statements, and this information must be included in interim as well as annual financial statements, contrary to the previous practice of providing pro forma disclosures only in annual financial statements.

This change probably will cause some companies debating whether to adopt Statement 123 in 2003 or 2004 to accelerate their adoption plans. However, it appears that most companies are still in the information-gathering mode. They are assessing the impact on their financial statements and compensation strategy as well as awaiting the results of the IASB's project on stock-based accounting and the potential impact that it might have on U.S. accounting requirements.

# Index

# About the Authors

## Alan A. Nadel

Alan is a partner with Ernst & Young LLP in New York City, practicing in the area of compensation and benefits. He advises clients about executive and board of directors' compensation, employee benefits, retirement benefit programs, and income and estate planning. He is frequently consulted on the various aspects of these arrangements, including the strategic, financial, accounting and tax considerations. He is a frequent speaker before professional and industry groups and is often quoted in the business press. Alan is a Certified Public Accountant and a former Internal Revenue Agent. He holds graduate degrees in actuarial science from New York University and in taxation from Bernard Baruch College, and an undergraduate degree in mathematics from John Carroll University. He is a co-author of the *Employee Benefits Handbook*. Alan serves on the board of directors of the American Benefits Council and the Certified Equity Professional Institute. His editorial board affiliations include the *Compensation Planning Journal, Journal of Compensation and Benefits,* and *Executive Compensation Developments.*

## Thomas M. Haines

Tom is a shareholder and head of the Chicago office of Frederic W. Cook & Co., where he has over 13 years of board-level consulting experience in the design and implementation of executive and outside director compensation programs. Tom's consulting experience extends over a broad range of company sizes and industries, and includes projects such as total compensation reviews, annual and long-term incentive plan designs, special retention arrangements, new hire and retirement/resignation packages, and equity conversions and change-in-control provisions in connection with business acquisitions and divestitures. Tom is the firm's technical expert in the areas of federal tax law and U.S. accounting standards as they pertain to executive compensation, and he is a frequent speaker and writer on these topics. Tom is a member of the teaching faculty at WorldatWork (formerly the American Compensation Association) where he teaches advanced courses on executive compensation to industry professionals. Tom also oversees the firm's propriety survey database of long-term incentive awards. Tom is a Certified Public Accountant (CPA) with a Masters degree in business taxation (MBT) from the University of Minnesota and a Bachelors degree in business accounting from the University of St. Thomas.

## Gregory M. Kopp

Greg is a senior manager with Deloitte & Touche in New York City, practicing in the area of executive compensation and equity incentives. He has 15 years of experience providing executive compensation consulting services to a wide range of public and privately held organizations in diverse industries. Greg has a broad range of experience in compensation consulting, including designing executive pay programs, board compensation programs, broad-based equity programs, severance arrangements, and employment contracts. Additionally, Greg has provided compensation consulting services to companies in transactional situations (e.g., merger and acquisition, divestiture, and bankruptcy). Greg has presented at conferences on various compensation-related subjects and has written articles for publication in domestic and international periodicals on topics including U.S. compensation design and accounting for executive compensation programs. Greg received a B.B.A degree in finance from Pace University and has graduate level studies in Fordham University's MBA program. Greg is also a Certified Financial Planner.

# About the NCEO

The National Center for Employee Ownership (NCEO) is widely considered to be the leading authority in employee ownership in the U.S. and the world. Established in 1981 as a nonprofit information and membership organization, it now has over 3,000 members, including companies, professionals, unions, government officials, academics, and interested individuals. It is funded entirely through the work it does.

The NCEO's mission is to provide the most objective, reliable information possible about employee ownership at the most affordable price possible. As part of the NCEO's commitment to providing objective information, it does not lobby or provide ongoing consulting services. The NCEO publishes a variety of materials on employee ownership and participation, and holds dozens of workshops and conferences on employee ownership annually. The NCEO's work includes extensive contacts with the media, both through articles written for trade and professional publications and through interviews with reporters. It has written or edited five books for outside publishers during the past two decades. Finally, the NCEO maintains an extensive Web site at *www.nceo.org*, plus a site on global equity-based compensation at *www.nceoglobal.org*.

# Membership Benefits

NCEO members receive the following benefits:

- The bimonthly newsletter, *Employee Ownership Report*, which covers ESOPs, stock options, and employee participation.
- Access to the members-only area of the NCEO's Web site, which includes a searchable database of well over 200 NCEO members who are service providers in this field.
- Substantial discounts on publications and events produced by the NCEO (such as this book).
- The right to telephone the NCEO for answers to general or specific questions regarding employee ownership.

An introductory NCEO membership costs $80 for one year ($90 outside the U.S.) and covers an entire company at all locations, a single office of a firm offering professional services in this field, or an individual with a business interest in employee ownership. Full-time students and faculty members who are not employed in the business sector may join at the academic rate of $35 for one year ($45 outside the U.S.).

# Selected NCEO Publications

The NCEO offers a variety of publications on all aspects of employee ownership and participation. Following are descriptions of our main publications.

We publish new books and revise old ones on a yearly basis. To obtain the most current information on what we have available, visit our extensive Web site at *www.nceo.org* or call us at 510-208-1300.

### Stock Options and Related Plans

- This book, *Accounting for Equity Compensation*, is a guide to the financial accounting rules that govern equity compensation programs in the United States.

    $35 for NCEO members, $50 for nonmembers

- *The Stock Options Book* is a straightforward, comprehensive over-view covering the legal, accounting, regulatory, and design issues involved in implementing a stock option or stock purchase plan. It is our main book on the subject.

  $25 for NCEO members, $35 for nonmembers .

- *Selected Issues in Stock Options* is more detailed and specialized than *The Stock Options Book,* with chapters on issues such as repricing, securities issues, and evergreen options. The appendix is an exhaustive glossary of terms used in the field.

  $25 for NCEO members, $35 for nonmembers

- *Beyond Stock Options* is a guide to phantom stock, stock appreciation rights, restricted stock, direct stock purchase plans, and performance awards used as alternatives to stock options. Includes a CD with model plans.

  $35 for NCEO members, $50 for nonmembers

- *Equity Compensation in a Post-Expensing World* is a collection of essays on strategies for choosing and structuring equity compensation plans when expensing is required.

  $25 for NCEO members, $35 for nonmembers

- *The Employee's Guide to Stock Options* is a guide for the everyday employee that explains in an easy-to-understand format what stock is and how stock options work.

  $25 for both NCEO members and nonmembers

- *Communicating Stock Options* offers practical ideas and information about how to explain stock options to a broad group of employees. It includes both essays and sample communication materials.

  $35 for NCEO members, $50 for nonmembers

- *Employee Stock Purchase Plans* covers how ESPPs work, tax and legal issues, administration, accounting, communicating the plan to employees, and research on what companies are doing with their plans.

  $25 for NCEO members, $35 for nonmembers

- *Model Equity Compensation Plans* provides examples of incentive stock option, nonqualified stock option, and stock purchase plans, together with brief explanations of the main documents. A disk is included with copies of the plan documents in formats any word processing program can open.

    $50 for NCEO members, $75 for nonmembers

- *Current Practices in Stock Option Plan Design* is a highly detailed report on our survey of companies with broad-based stock option plans conducted in 2000. It includes a detailed examination of plan design, use, and experience broken down by industry, size, and other categories.

    $25 for NCEO members, $35 for nonmembers

- *Stock Options, Corporate Performance, and Organizational Change* presents the first serious research to examine the relationship between broadly granted stock options and company performance, and the extent of employee involvement in broad option companies.

    $15 for NCEO members, $25 for nonmembers

- *Equity-Based Compensation for Multinational Corporations* describes how companies can use stock options and other equity-based programs across the world to reward a global work force. It includes a country-by-country summary of tax and legal issues as well as a detailed case study.

    $25 for NCEO members, $35 for nonmembers

- *Incentive Compensation and Employee Ownership* takes a broad look at how companies can use incentives, ranging from stock plans to cash bonuses to gainsharing, to motivate and reward employees. It includes both technical discussions and case studies.

    $25 for NCEO members, $35 for nonmembers

## Employee Stock Ownership Plans (ESOPs)

- *The ESOP Reader* is an overview of the issues involved in establishing and operating an ESOP. It covers the basics of ESOP rules, feasibility, valuation, and other matters, and then discusses managing an ESOP company, including brief case studies. The book is intended for those with a general interest in ESOPs.

$25 for NCEO members, $35 for nonmembers

- *Selling to an ESOP* is a guide for owners, managers, and advisors of closely held businesses. It explains how ESOPs work and then offers a comprehensive look at legal structures, valuation, financing (including self-financing), and other matters, especially the tax-deferred section 1042 "rollover" that allows owners to indefinitely defer capital gains taxation on the proceeds of the sale to the ESOP.

$25 for NCEO members, $35 for nonmembers

- *Leveraged ESOPs and Employee Buyouts* discusses how ESOPs borrow money to buy out entire companies, purchase shares from a retiring owner, or finance new capital. Beginning with a primer on leveraged ESOPs and their uses, it then discusses contribution limits, valuation, accounting, feasibility studies, financing sources, and more.

$25 for NCEO members, $35 for nonmembers

- The *Model ESOP* contains a sample ESOP plan, with alternative provisions given to tailor the plan to individual needs. It also includes a section-by-section explanation of the plan and other supporting materials.

$50 for NCEO members, $75 for nonmembers

- *ESOP Valuation* brings together and updates where needed the best articles on ESOP valuation that we have published in our *Journal of Employee Ownership Law and Finance,* described below.

$25 for NCEO members, $35 for nonmembers

- The *Employee Ownership Q&A Disk* gives Microsoft Windows users (any version from Windows 3.1 onward) point-and-click access to 500 questions and answers on all aspects of ESOPs in a fully searchable hypertext format.

$75 for NCEO members, $100 for nonmembers

- *How ESOP Companies Handle the Repurchase Obligation* is a short publication with articles and research on the subject.

  $10 for NCEO members, $15 for nonmembers

- *The ESOP Committee Guide* describes the different types of ESOP committees, the range of goals they can address, alternative structures, member selection criteria, training, committee life cycle concerns, and other issues.

  $25 for NCEO members, $35 for nonmembers

- *Wealth and Income Consequences of Employee Ownership* is a detailed report on a comparative study of ESOP companies in Washington State that found ESOP companies pay more and provided better benefits than other companies.

  $10 for NCEO members, $15 for nonmembers

- The *ESOP Communications Sourcebook* is a publication for ESOP companies with ideas and examples on how to communicate an ESOP to employees and market employee ownership to customers.

  $35 for NCEO members, $50 for nonmembers

## Employee Involvement and Management

- *Ownership Management* draws upon the experience of the NCEO and of leading employee ownership companies to discuss how to build a culture of lasting innovation by combining employee ownership with employee involvement programs. It includes specific ideas on how to structure programs and get employees involved.

  $25 for NCEO members, $35 for nonmembers

- *Front Line Finance Facilitator's Manual* gives step-by-step instructions for teaching business literacy, emphasizing ESOPs.

  $50 for NCEO members, $75 for nonmembers

- *Front Line Finance Diskette* contains the workbook for participants in electronic form (so a copy can be printed out for everyone) in the *Front Line Finance* course.

  $50 for NCEO members, $75 for nonmembers

- *Cultural Diversity and Employee Ownership* discusses how companies with employee stock plans deal with diversity and communicate employee ownership.

  $25 for NCEO members, $35 for nonmembers

## Other

- *Section 401(k) Plans and Employee Ownership* focuses on how company stock is used in 401(k) plans, both in stand-alone 401(k) plans and combination 401(k)–ESOP plans ("KSOPs").

  $25 for NCEO members, $35 for nonmembers

- *A Conceptual Guide to Equity-Based Compensation for Non-U.S. Companies* helps companies outside the U.S. think through how to approach employee ownership.

  $25 for NCEO members, $35 for nonmembers

- *The Journal of Employee Ownership Law and Finance* is the only professional journal solely devoted to employee ownership. Articles are written by leading experts and cover ESOPs, stock options, and related subjects in depth.

  One-year subscription (four issues):
  $75 for NCEO members, $100 for nonmembers

**To join the NCEO as a member or to order any of the publications listed on the preceding pages, use the order form on the following page, use the secure ordering system on our Web site at www.nceo.org, or call us at 510-208-1300. If you join at the same time you order publications, you will receive the members-only publication discounts.**

# Order Form

To order, fill out this form and mail it with your credit card information or check to the NCEO at 1736 Franklin St., 8th Flr., Oakland, CA 94612; fax it with your credit card information to the NCEO at 510-272-9510; telephone us at 510-208-1300 with your credit card in hand; or order at our Web site, *www.nceo.org.* If you are not already a member, you can join now to receive member discounts on any publications you order.

Name

Organization

Address

City, State, Zip (Country)

Telephone          Fax          E-mail

**Method of Payment:** ❑ Check (payable to "NCEO")    ❑ Visa    ❑ M/C    ❑ AMEX

Credit Card Number

Signature          Exp. Date

| Title | Qty. | Price | Total |
|-------|------|-------|-------|
|       |      |       |       |
|       |      |       |       |
|       |      |       |       |
|       |      |       |       |

**Tax:** California residents add 8.25% sales tax (on publications only, not membership or Journal subscriptions)

**Shipping:** In the U.S., first publication $5, each add'l $1; elsewhere, we charge exact shipping costs to your credit card, plus (except for Canada) a $10 handling surcharge; no shipping charges for membership or Journal subscriptions

**Introductory NCEO Membership:** $80 for one year ($90 outside the U.S.)

| | |
|--|--|
| Subtotal | $ |
| Sales Tax | $ |
| Shipping | $ |
| Membership | $ |
| TOTAL DUE | $ |